Bridges to Accessibility

Mark D. Havens

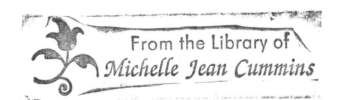

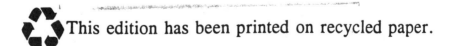
This edition has been printed on recycled paper.

Project Adventure, Inc.

Dedication

This primer is dedicated to the individuals I have worked *with*, who have disabilities that are visually apparent. Through this process of *working with*, I have become more aware of my own disabilities, which were hidden from view.

Acknowledgments

I was fortunate, early in my career, to have three mentors. Gary Robb encouraged me to take risks as a practitioner — even when those risks could have affected his own career. Gerald Fain encouraged me to be reflective in practice and modeled this behavior quite often in my presence. Tom Smith encouraged me to take my own personal growth as seriously as those I worked with. Without the mentoring of these individuals, I would not have had the experiences to write this primer. Thank You.

I would also like to thank the Staff at Project Adventure for supporting and nurturing this project along. Dick Prouty and Tom Zierk deserve a great deal of credit for this product and I appreciated their constant reminders to write from the heart. A special thanks goes to Bonnie Hannable for her thorough editing of the manuscript. Moreover, it is a great benefit to be able to work with colleagues who are also your friends. I thank Bill Quinn, Erik Marter, Christopher Roland, Judy Hoyt, Dale Abell, John Galland, Jill Pergande, Steve Brannan, Janet Sable, Dan Creely, Sunny Ku, Karen Overton and many others for their support over the years.

Finally, I would like to say THANKS to my family who are always excited and interested in what I am doing, even during those periods when "what I'm doing" is not that exciting!

Contents

Foreword

"Our disability is our opportunity."...Kurt Hahn

This phrase, made famous by Kurt Hahn, the founder of Outward Bound in England, is used by many Adventure program leaders. But it now takes on new meaning. Traditionally, we have used the quote to help individuals reframe issues and seize opportunities for growth. However, the principle issue that this book begins to address is not primarily a participant issue. The greater issue is that as Adventure program leaders, we must recognize how much better we can get at embracing and guiding the full participation of all persons, including those with "disabilities."

Adventure programming has great strengths that can be used to bring people together. Previous books published by Project Adventure and by others demonstrate the ability of well executed Adventure experiences to forge a common ground. The attributes of the successful Adventure learning program are becoming increasingly well known: the ability to set challenging goals, to take risks to accomplish those goals, to experience the problem solving value of play and fun, all within the supportive atmosphere of the group. One measure of Adventure programming's acceptance is its inclusion within so many different disciplines and institutions. Many of people who successfully use Adventure as a learning tool are those who specialize in helping defined populations, be it those with chemical dependence, head injuries or other issues that place them in need of assistance.

But the trend gathering steam now, especially with the new Americans with Disabilities Act of 1991, is that most of our programs will increasingly be dealing with a more diverse grouping of people. Integrated community-based programming is becoming more accessible and potentially more successful at reaching all persons. The theory and research here is clear on one point: *if* a diverse group is functioning well, it has more creativity and learning available to it than does a group of less diversity. In that *if* lies the challenge and opportunity for our field.

Our Adventure bag of tricks gives us a leg up on making a group work well. But, as Mark makes clear in this book, the major barrier to effective programming for people from more diverse backgrounds is the attitude and interpersonal skills of the facilitator/leader. All of us in the Adventure and helping fields need to examine our own attitudes, and by working with participants and relevant specialists, make our own particular programs truly universal in scope. *Bridges To Accessibility* is a start in addressing that need.

We at Project Adventure, along with many of you we hope, will be working to make sure that the Adventure field addresses this important issue with all the strengths at its command. We will be looking to ourselves as well. We will address our own preconceptions and attitudes about people with disabilities and learning with you and from you as we address this issue. The payoff will be richer and more valuable learning experiences for all of us.

Dick Prouty

Project Adventure, Inc.

Preface

To this day, I can still remember my first Adventure experience. It was the Summer of 1978. I can recall the specific ropes course elements used, the people who participated with me, and the course facilitators (along with their leadership styles). More importantly, I remember the impact the experience had on me...personally. As with most people who have had a significant experience, I was motivated to hurry back to the place I was working (a camp for children and adults with disabilities), and talk non-stop about how Adventure programming could impact the lives of the campers — and it did.

From that summer on, I have worked at making Adventure experiences accessible with individuals who are disabled. As I look back on my career, I am not sure whether my primary motivation was to help myself or persons with disabilities. However, I do know that I was doing what I "felt" was the right thing to do. In fact, I still continue to have the same enthusiasm for Adventure learning and working "with" persons who are disabled. I also constantly remind myself to reflect on my primary motivation for practice.

As a helper, I have been trained to advocate for and provide services which have not been readily available to individuals who are disabled. Such is the case with community-based Adventure programs. My drive to found and operate Accessible Adventures came from a desire to make ropes/challenge courses and related curricula accessible. However, times have changed!

The majority of individuals with disabilities live in the community. Therefore, the need for "specialized" companies and/or segregated programs are, in my opinion, on the way out. I am aware of the need for and the existence of several quality "specialized" programs. Yet, the time for integrated community-based Adventure programming is long overdue.

My rationale for writing this primer is based on four personal beliefs: First, I am convinced that, as a Therapeutic Recreation Specialist and a "specialized"

Adventure business owner, I can be more effective by collaborating with companies like Project Adventure, who provide community-based Adventure programs on a grand scale. This collaboration will help in providing safe and effective integrated Adventure programs on the community level; second, I believe that the more diverse the participants are, in any group, the more fruitful the experience; third, I hope that, as Adventure leaders, we can learn more when we program with persons who have a broad range of ages, origins, interests and abilities; and fourth, I believe that integration does enhance acceptance!

I hope this primer will stimulate awareness among community-based Adventure leaders toward the inclusion of persons with disabilities in their on-going programs. Concurrently, my desire is that the content will encourage "specialists" to collaborate more with community-based Adventure leaders and programs so the opportunities for integration become more of a reality.

Finally, I struggled with "proper language" for this publication. I made an effort to focus on emphasizing "people" before disability. The word "challenge" is used quite often in the text. I know some people with disabilities find the word "challenge" offensive; e.g., challenges are something people choose. However, since there is no consensus on proper language, I chose to use a variety of word combinations. With all of this in mind, I hope the reader will appreciate my attempt to be *non-handicapist* in my use of the written word.

Introduction

*"Adult survival, just as with children, is more and more
dependent upon our understanding and accepting humankind
in all of its varieties." (Bower, 1980, p.v)*

The primary purpose of this primer is to encourage the reader to include persons with disabilities in the many benefits which can be gleaned from on-going Adventure programs. Otherwise, I hope the community Adventure leaders will be motivated to learn more about people with disabilities and feel comfortable welcoming them into their programs. Also, it is my intention to provide the "specialist" with a document that can assist them in advocating for integrated Adventure programming. The content should not be mistaken for a how-to or "cookbook" for programming with people who are disabled. Bri*dges To Accessibility* is a primer or more succinctly, a beginning point of awareness for society at large.

There is a great deal of justification for this primer. The last two decades have brought legal action and legislation which mandate integration in educational, recreational and vocational settings. The process of deinstitutionalization has placed many individuals with disabilities back in the community to live, work and play. Moreover, the barriers or obstacles to participation by persons with disabilities, in community Adventure programs, are no longer insurmountable.

It is time to support the integration of Adventure experiences. While many have begun this effort, the ractice is not common. This primer should encourage readers to *want*" to make their services accessible — not just react to a legislative mandate. It should encourage the specialist to collaborate with and support the community Adventure leader so safe and effective integrated programs become a reality. The content is centered on attitudinal awareness. However, there is information included which can begin to prepare the reader to respond proactively to the coming of integration and mainstreaming within the context of Adventure education.

I would hope that, after reading this primer, the reader will agree with me on several ideas. First, that empowerment is the most effective process for facilitating personal growth with all people. This process must begin with the facilitator (via therapy, reflective practice, etc.).

Second, that the traditional "clinical/medical model" training of specialists is incomplete. Although necessary in some cases, additional skills and attitude awareness are required to help move from prescriptive leadership to empowering practice.

And third, that the principles behind Adventure learning require the facilitator to encourage independence and self-discovery among all participants. Consequently, if Adventure education is utilized with persons who are disabled — in integrated settings — it is only natural to promote and model personal responsibility. Overprotectiveness, creating dependence among participants, etc., are no longer acceptable leadership behaviors.

I do anticipate that this primer will create additional questions that need answering, stimulate more issues to be addressed, but hopefully and most importantly, inspire others to "build more bridges to accessibility."

Section One provides background information on how individuals with disabilities have been treated or perceived throughout history (including their involvement in Adventure programs) and a synthesis of the factors which have moved our society towards integration. A brief history of accessible Adventure is provided in order to give the reader a context. A rationale for integration, legislative realities, and problems with labelling are discussed.

Section Two presents an overview of exceptionality with implications and opportunities for Adventure leaders. In this section, I have included several observations, learned from experience, that can help leaders make the Adventure accessible for individuals with specific disabilities.

Section Three focuses on information for "building bridges" and challenges the individual Adventure programmer to assess his or her own skills and attitudes for the effective inclusion of persons with disabilities. Also included is accessible Adventure curricula. This chapter, 7, provides examples of what can be done to make Adventure accessible. A summary of suggestions and opportunities for moving forward concludes this section.

The appendicies provide more specific information which will assist the leader in being proactive in the transition from segregation to integration. Included in the appendices are resources (e.g., movies, books, magazines, and organizations that can foster integrated Adventure experiences); surveys to determine personal attitude awareness and the accessibility of Adventure programs and facilities; safety considerations; key definitions and terms; sample resources for training; and information on what Project Adventure can do to assist all Adventure leaders.

Section One

BACKGROUND

The concepts of integration and mainstreaming are not new. However, the practice of involving persons with disabilities in the day-to-day events that go on in communities is; i.e., education, recreation, religious and political. Consequently, few children and adults who are disabled participate in community-based Adventure programs.

This section will assist the reader in understanding some historical implications that have led to a lack of integration and mainstreaming within the context of adventure and related programs. The section also provides a look forward using examples of integrated Adventure experiences that support social interaction and acceptance for all.

A brief history of accessible Adventure is included with the purpose of placing the contents of this primer in perspective for the Adventure leader. Finally, a rationale for mainstreaming Adventure programs is proposed along with past and current legislation that supports the notion that integration does enhance acceptance.

Chapter One

History

I am convinced that Adventure programs — in their many forms — are here to stay. People, across many nations, are involved in Adventure curricula which challenge individuals to take more risks, small groups to function more effectively and entire organizations to be more productive. However, there are a significant number of individuals — with disabilities — who are "missing" from many community-based Adventure experiences. If every citizen has a right to access all community services; e.g., medical, religious and educational, then the Adventure experience should be accessible as well. It is time for Adventure leaders to consider the inclusion of persons with disabilities in community-based Adventure programs — not just via a physical presence but with social interaction and acceptance.

Looking Back

Persons with disabilities have seldom been valorized (valued) in society. In fact, most persons with disabilities have inherited inferior roles that can be traced back through time and are still present today. Wolfensberger (1972, 1985) has eloquently reported on persons who are considered deviant by society when they have a significant physical difference which is negatively valued. According to Wolfensberger

(1972), "When a person is perceived as a deviant, he is cast into a role that carries with it powerful expectations. Strangely enough, these expectations not only take hold of the mind of the perceiver but of the perceived person as well." (p.15). In other words, the persons with disabilities tend to perceive themselves as outside of social norms and, therefore, "deviant."

It is important for Adventure program leaders to acknowledge how these historic roles often dictate societal attitudes. Many pre-scribed role models influence the personal perspective of able-bodied participants as well as people with disabilities. The following roles have been reported in Wolfensberger's' book, *Normalization: The Principle of Normalization in Human Services*, (1972).

A Subhuman Organism

Have you ever heard someone refer to a person with a disability as a "vegetable?" It is comments like these that deprive people with disabilities full value as human beings. To quote Wolfensberger (1972, p.17) ...a comment in the *Atlantic Monthly* (October, 1967, p. 49) called for '...sacrifice of mentally defective humans, or human vegetables...to provide organ transplants and ...increase the intellectual betterment of mankind...'.

A Menace

Historically, society has tended to attribute evil to any "differentness," regardless of whether it is physical, behavioral or intellectual. Consider the fact that many movies and some holidays (Halloween for example) portray people with disabilities as scary or evil.

Object of Pity

In soliciting funds for an organization who provides services for children who are autistic, a newspaper ran an advertisement showing a child sitting in front of his birthday cake with four candles. The heading read, "Johnny will be four years old for the rest of his life...won't you help?" There may be benevolence and compassion in this form of public service ad. It also, however, communicates to the general public a lack of respect and hope for the child with the disability.

A Holy Innocent

The word "special" is applied to many programs and service organiza-tions that support persons with disabilities. This word can affect how we perceive children and adults with disabilities, sometimes exempt-ing full expectations for behavioral responsibility and applying child-like qualities to adults. This can be a barrier to promoting personal

independence — a goal of many special and Adventure programs. I have oftentimes over-spotted or over protected participants with disabilities on ropes courses for fear that they may get hurt and the program might get cancelled. This behavior takes away from their experience and minimizes their independence. Consequently, I have to work on my own fears and need to control.

A Diseased Organism

An athlete, a marathoner who uses a wheel-chair, attempted to join a health club. The manager told the athlete that the facility was not a rehabilitation center. The athlete was a woman who had completed five marathons in under two and one-half hours. She did not need therapy, she simply needed access to the facility and equipment.

An Object of Ridicule

People with disabilities were employed as court jesters or fools during the medieval period (Wolfensberger, 1972). During more recent times, circus companies have gener-ated profits by capitalizing on the public's curiosity for viewing people who are different, thus perpetuating a zoo-like perspective and atmosphere.

It is important for the Adventure leader to acknowledge how these historic roles often dictate societal attitudes. The majority of individuals with disabilities do not require therapeutic Adventure programs, they simply need access to the adventure.

An Eternal Child

When society perceives people with disabilities as being incapable of becoming independent, we exclude the possibility of them having developmental or adaptational qualities. Too often, we alter the environment to compensate for a person's disabilities rather than recognizing her capabilities and adapting the environment to support and enhance those strengths. I have built many "specialized" ropes courses that have been effective in segregated environments. However, I hope this primer leads to the creation of more accessible courses within integrated environments.

Adventure curricula has many common themes such as: learning to set realistic goals, building trust in ourselves and others, and learning to be playful. In addition, individual participants are encour-aged to assess problem solving skills both individually and as group members. It is believed that these exercises improve the participants' abilities to take physical, emotional, and intellectual risks. Persons with disabilities benefit equally from these important Adventure programming themes. However, if leaders in the Adventure field subscribe to antiquated perspectives (limited abilities) towards persons with disabilities, there is danger of:

- perceiving some members of our society as not fully human;
- having a narrow perspective of what is beautiful, right or good;
- allowing sympathy or pity to override feelings of empathy;
- not expecting "the best effort" from each participant in our programs;
- not empowering individuals...feeling overly responsible or protective;
- perceiving some members as "trivial," or less important; and,
- not affording all members of society an opportunity for independence.

Looking Forward

Who would have imagined, that by the year 1990, the Adventure experience would be a major topic of interest in education, recreation, treatment and corporate settings? The content of Adventure education (curricula) comes in many forms and is often tailored to meet the specific needs of a particular group. To explore these many forms is beyond the scope of this primer. However, Schoel, Prouty and Radcliffe, in *Islands of Healing* (1988), provide a much used sequence of Adventure activities that will serve as a general foundation for this primer. They include:

Trust Exercises, leading to Trust Falls and Spotting, which develop attentiveness, risk taking, empathy, cooperation, and group spirit.

Games, which develop a sense of fun and cooperation.

Problem-Solving Exercises, which develop individual and group initiative, spirit, independence and competence.

Ropes Course Experiences, which encourage trust, risk and empathy.

Community Service and Learning Projects, which develop a sense

It is important for the Adventure leader to expect "the best effort" from all participants in Adventure programs.

of caring and connectedness to the world at large.

Expeditions, extended forays, either for several hours, days or weeks into "foreign" territory, which compress the above outcomes and reinforce them in an intense, mutual peak experience (p. x–xi).

This primer is about the use of Adventure activities and experiences. More specifically, though, it is about the estimated 40 million Americans, with disabilities, who have not typically had access to Adventure experiences, especially in integrated settings. The majority of individuals who are considered disabled live in communities, yet few use traditional community resources.

Persons with physical, emotional and intellectual challenges have lived, worked, recreated and hve attended school in segregated environments. It was the philosophy of many that such individuals would be happier and more appropriately cared for by specially trained professionals in protective environments (institutions). The times have changed!

The Community Marathon Project (a service learning activity which is present in most Adventure curricula) is what this primer is all about; it involves the process of making Adventure education accessible.

Moving Towards Integration

Joanne Maynard is a Special Needs Teacher at Marblehead High School, in Marblehead, Massachusetts, and is a Certified Project Adventure Trainer. More importantly, she is a "change agent." She is the prime mover behind the Community Marathon: Students working together for change. The players behind this project are a group of regular and special education students who came together to, "Learn about each other, learn about AIDS and earn money for direct AIDS care." The Community Marathon (a walking event) involves people from the community participating in a fundraising effort to support direct AIDS care.

The "process" Joanne has initiated involves Adventure learning; e.g., the use of a community service and learning project within an integrated group — students with different abilities. Additionally, this diverse group, through the use of Adventure education, summoned a goal statement which reads, "We don't want to be afraid of differences. We are committed to learn and appreciate more about diversity in our school and community and work toward valuing them." This example represents a "bridge to accessibility."

Opportunities for integration in Adventure programming are escalating as society opens more doors for disabled and able-bodied persons to interact in risk-taking environments. It is not at all uncommon to hear professionals in the human service arena support the notion that integration enhances acceptance. To effectively rise to the challenge of integration and mainstreaming in Adventure learning environments, it is imperative to prepare leaders to: a), utilize both the "technical" and "facilitation" skills necessary to accommodate groups enjoying a wide continuum of abilities; b), engage in accessible trust exercises, cooperative games, problem-solving experiences, ropes course elements, community service/learning projects, and expeditions; and c), promote the transition from segregated to integrated Adventure programming while maintaining emotional, physical and intellectual safety for all.

A Brief History of Accessible Adventure

This brief historical review of accessible Adventure is not intended to be a detailed account of the development of access to integrated programming with persons who are disabled. I am aware that the history is not well documented and understand that many important events occurred before or simultaneously to the content included in this review. Many individuals, both lay and professional, have been instrumental in providing and advocating for challenging activities with persons who are disabled. This account is an attempt to place accessible Adventure programming in perspective. I apologize, in advance, if events or people have been excluded; moreover, I encourage further study in this area.

According to Schleien & Ray (1988), "The origin of therapeutic wilderness programs in the early 1900's in the United States was chronicled in the American Journal of Insanity..." (p.4). For the nearly eight decades that followed, persons with disabilities participated in primarily segregated camping and outdoor recreation experiences.

Segregated programs in recreation and outdoor education began through the advocacy of parents of persons with disabilities who were not able to place their children in community based programs. Agencies such as the Muscular Dystrophy Association, Easter Seal Society, United Cerebral Palsy Association, etc., grew out of a need for services which were not available in most communities. Key events have led to the involvement of persons with disabilities in Adventure and outdoor recreation experiences; some of which include:

1940–1970 — Establishment of several organizations that have outdoor recreation as a component; e.g., the Paralyzed Veterans of America (PVA), National Wheelchair Athletic Association (NWAA), and the North American Riding for the Handicapped Association (NARHA).

1970's — Federal funding of several projects focusing on outdoor education, recreation and camping for persons with disabilities; e.g., Project TORCH: Training Personnel in Outdoor Education, Recreation and Camping with the Handicapped, Indiana University, and EXPLORE: Expanding Leisure Opportunities in Outdoor Recreation, Portland State University.

1980's — National conferences and workshops on outdoor recreation with persons who are disabled. Examples are The Bradford Institute at Indiana University and Innovations To Access, Boston University.

The Tree Climb Program

Camp Allen is a camp for children and adults with disabilities located in Bedford, New Hampshire. In 1977, I was the Physical Recreation Director and Gary Robb was the Director. Together we explored the idea of an Adventure program for the summer sessions. We contracted with Christopher Roland to build a high platform, in a tree, which could be used as a beginning Adventure experience. Campers could be either hoisted (if physically disabled) or could take one of the many climbing routes to the platform.

The platform was constructed and staff were trained to operate the activity. Approximately 200 campers participated in the "Tree Climb Program" with a great deal of enthusiasm and success.

From 1977–1981, "Tree Climb Programs" were implemented at Bradford Woods (Indiana University's Outdoor Education Center) in Martinsville, Indiana; Camp Millhouse (a camp for persons with disabilities) in South Bend, Indiana; and at other camps and outdoor centers that traditionally served children and youth with disabilities. Concurrently, Chris Roland and I published an article in *Camping Magazine* (January, 1982) entitled, *"Tree Climbing: Handicapped Find Perch Exciting."*

From this beginning, Chris and I explored the possibility of adapting existing Project Adventure ropes/challenge course elements

to serve both children and adults with disabilities. In 1981, Dale Abell, who was employed by the Vinland National Center (a Center which provides health-sports programs and curricula for persons who are disabled), contracted with us to construct an accessible ropes/challenge course at the Vinland National Center in Loretto, Minnesota. During the summer of 1981, an interdisciplinary team of both able-bodied and disabled persons completed an accessible challenge course. In that same year, Chris and I completed a manual entitled, *An Introduction To Adventure: A Sequential Approach To Challenging Activities With Persons Who Are Disabled*, which was edited by Dale Abell and published by the Vinland National Center.

The Tree Climb Program was simple, but it opened the door for many individuals with disabilities to take risks.

In 1981, accessible challenge courses were built at Bradford Woods, Mt. Hood Kiwanis Camp, in Rhododendron, Oregon, Kamp for Kids, in Westfield, Massachusetts, The Cotting School (an indoor accessible course), in Boston, Hemlocks Outdoor Education Center, in Hebron, Connecticut, and at other camps, schools and outdoor centers across the United States.

Project Interdependence was a federally funded effort to develop strategies to integrate persons with disabilities into various California educational and recreational programs. By the mid 1980's, it had established many successful integrations and had worked extensively with Adventure-based applications. Ted Fay was the Project Director and worked often with Reno Taini, a teacher in a public school alternative program with an extensive background in Adventure programming. The basic philosophy of Project Interdependence, that persons of various disabilities could (should) be encouraged to work together in groups to solve problems together, and that all parties could learn from each other, was ahead of its time and blazed significant new ground.

Another program that deserves mention is Camp Courageous of Iowa, which believes that "disabled individuals, as well as their families, should experience year-round recreational and respite care activities in a camp setting...and provides this needed service to all." Founded in 1972, the camp built a confidence course in 1976 and currently serves over 3,000 campers annually, ranging in ages from 1 to 100! With a camper to staff ratio that frequently runs 1 to 1, Camp Courageous offers Challenge Course elements such as a Burma Bridge, an Adapted Tree Climb, Cable Ladder and Indoor Climbing Wall. The camp also offers extended canoeing and bicycling trips.

During the 1980's, much of the Adventure curricula — awareness, goal setting, trust development, cooperative games, individual and group problem solving, community service projects and wilderness travel — was a popular theme in terms of making this medium accessible to persons with disabilities. Gary Robb, Tom Smith, Greg Lais, Jeffrey Witman, John Galland, Steve Brannan, Dale Abell, Judith Hoyt and many others have written and continue to write extensively on the need, rationale for, and effectiveness of integrating Adventure curricula. (See Appendix A: Resource Section, for a detailed list of movies, books, articles and organizations supporting the concept that "integration enhances acceptance.")

A Case Study

The following historical outline, contributed by Pam McPhee at the University of New Hampshire, highlights an example of the emergence of accessible Adventure.

Accessible Adventure at UNH

by Pam McPhee

The University of New Hampshire has offered a major in Outdoor Education since 1983. As part of this major, students, in conjunction with Project Adventure, built a challenge course in 1987. Since that time, UNH has been offering ropes courses as part of its training for the outdoor education students and as a community service. We presently serve approximately 2,000 individuals per year.

In May of 1987, as I waited for a group of UNH Students to arrive, I thumbed through the medical forms noting nothing unusual except that one form was missing. Within minutes the group arrived and the missing form was found in the lap of Leslie Washburn who had arrived with the group in her motorized wheelchair (she has muscular dystrophy). With little more than a, "Sure, why not?" attitude, the day, and my first accessible ropes course experience, had started.

The first lesson I learned was that if I saw Leslie as a "person" in a chair that can't..., I might as well throw in the towel. Leslie is a dynamic individual with endless capabilities and this firmly established in my brain the idea that rules can be adapted with the assistance of all persons involved. Some examples of activities used that day include:

Name Game — Say your name, how you are feeling today, and if there is any physical or emotional concerns we, as a group, should be aware of today. This helped us realize that Leslie did feel comfortable being lifted from her chair when necessary.

The rules for many games and initiatives can be adapted to involve all participants. A little imagination and creativity can go a long way.

Pass the Hoola Hoop — We found it necessary to pass the hoop over heads and shoulders rather than around the entire body.

Willow in the Wind — We gave each other a big bear hug—front to front—I was responsible for the feet and she had the voice, so away we went, being passed around the circle.

Other activities that we made accessible on that day were Trust Falls from heights — using the bear hug approach, Spider's Web, high elements — where Leslie went up on another participant's back and belayed using a figure eight, and others that we made group challenges in order to solve the barriers to accessibility.

Since that day, much has happened. Motivated by a fundraising event (for Danny Burke, who has cerebral palsy), we were able to acquire funds for building accessible elements. A "come lend your ideas" day was held at UNH, where The High Trolley and five other elements were designed and built. Danny was the first to try the High Trolley (a large padded gym scooter locked and propelled by four pulleys on two parallel cables forty feet in the air). Danny, secured by "Danny's Sudan" — a hammock harness invented for full body and head support — was half way across the element on the maiden voyage when the entire contraption twisted and came off the cables. Nothing fell, but for a split second there was a possibility that the belay rope could get caught around Danny's neck. Danny was quickly lowered to the ground and within minutes wanted to try the element again. I was obviously still in shock and decided to re-think the course before we went forward.

At that point, I wanted to burn the entire course to the ground. Who was I to be endangering people? The answer that helped us all to go on with the course and make the necessary improvements came from Tim Churchard, a Project Adventure trainer. For the first time in his life, Danny had become a pioneer, someone who had accepted that real injury might result from the journey into the unknown, and he had chosen to take the risk.

Since that time, the challenge course has gone through many changes and continuous improvement. It is now integrated and provides challenges for everyone.

This honest and thoughtful contribution by Pam represents the struggles and risks many have taken in order to "build bridges to accessibility."

Several philosophical themes, which have had significant impact on the use of Adventure programs with persons who are disabled, are worth mentioning.

From Adapted to Accessible

With integration as a major focus, society has moved from providing separate, adapted programs and structures to offering accessible experiences and facilities. This parallels other undertakings such as:

- playgrounds for children with disabilities, which are being replaced by accessible playgrounds for all children
- braille nature trails for persons who are blind, which are being replaced by accessible nature trails with stations usable by all nature enthusiasts
- fitness parcourses for persons with disabilities, which are being replaced by fitness equipment and programs usable by people with different abilities.

Accessibility of the high elements for all persons ensures each participant is offered the whole adventure experience.

The result is an opportunity to enjoy the company of people with a wide continuum of physical, emotional, intellectual and spiritual abilities. Overall, we are moving towards the concept of "Universal Design," which promotes the consideration of all members of society when making structural and programmatic decisions.

Changing Professional Roles

Laws, such as P.L. 94–142 (Education of All Handicapped Children Act, 1975), have changed both our education and recreation philosophies and practices. For example, special education and allied health professionals are beginning to serve as consultants to the generic service providers in order to facilitate the transition of many persons who are disabled into integrated education and leisure environments.

Partnerships (Example)

Project Adventure — the largest provider of Adventure services — has encouraged the writing and publication of this "primer" to promote the concept of integration. This is testimony to a beginning awareness by society to begin to appreciate and value diversity.

Empowerment

The most effective action has been initiated by people with disabilities themselves. They are the major force behind many legislative activities and organizations promoting full inclusion in society. Don Rogers is the President of Pro Access, a consulting, training and design company focusing on providing challenging opportunities to people who are disabled. Consider this story by an individual who has made a difference for himself and others through Adventure education:

Personal Reflections

by Don Rogers

Life is colored with irony. Consider the passing of time. If we choose to do little with our time that is exciting and challenging, time seems to stagnate. However, if we choose to seek adventure in our lives, time speeds along as though it were an endless stream of consciousness.

No matter what our perceptions of time may be, the truth is we are in short supply. That motivates me to live each day to the fullest. On a fateful day, 15 years ago, I had a motorcycle accident that paralyzed my lower extremities and changed me as I knew myself. Since then, I've used a wheelchair to navigate through life; that is, when I'm not SCUBA diving, sky diving, snow skiing, etc.

In 1982, I went through the Minnesota Outward Bound School adapted course for people with disabilities. It was a 14-day course that consisted of canoeing, hiking, ropes course and a two-day solo. I didn't see God during my solo, but I did realize that I wanted to live a life that was this intense, a life that was challenging and where doubt about the outcome would keep me on my proverbial toes. Also, I wanted to help bring this quality of life to other people with disabilities as a professional in the Outdoor Adventure Field. It took little time to discover how few opportunities there were for persons like myself to participate in outdoor activities, commercially or otherwise, let alone find a job doing what I love. That's where the second half of the story begins.

I've been extremely fortunate to have friends along the way who share my thirst for adventure. Together we have created our own opportunities. After Outward Bound, I found myself in the high primitive area of the Uintah Mountains, east of Salt Lake City, with three other friends in chairs. We were all founding members of P.O.I.N.T. — Paraplegics On Independent Nature Trips. On this expedition, we each used a different make of wheelchair, experimenting with packing and pushing techniques. From this climb, we were able to design a chair that fit our back-country needs. The following summer, Quadra of California, built six of these chairs for us to use on our "assault" on Guadalupe Mountain, the highest peak in Texas at 8,751 feet. Three of us completed that climb, which precipitated a congratulatory call from President Reagan at a news conference held for us in Carlsbad, New Mexico.

Don Rogers has designed several accessible ropes/challenge course elements including the Rockin' Tri-Beams, Balance Platform, and the Ring Traverse.

Over the years that have followed, I've gone SCUBA diving, water skiing, sailing in the Gulf, sky diving, snow skiing, camping in the swamps of Caddo Lake, and fishing and camping every chance I can find.

Professionally, I've also been fortunate in forging opportunities. My goal is to be a professor in Therapeutic Recreation with an emphasis in outdoor applications. I hope that in January of 1992, I will begin a Ph.D. program at Indiana University. I currently have a Masters Degree in Outdoor Therapeutic Recreation from I.U. and a B.S. from the University of North Texas. Along the way, I've been trained and/or employed at a variety of agencies, such as the Vinland National Center, Dallas Parks and Recreation Bachman Center and at Bradford Woods. A strong combination of academic and experiential preparation is the key to a solid future in this field.

To look back on my life over the past 15 years is always a joy. Some would say I've been lucky or that good fortune has smiled upon me in misproportion. To that I say, luck is an overflow of hard work and fortune is not our destiny, it is a matter of our own choosing. My disability has not thrown opportunity at my feet, quite the opposite actually, which will always be my challenge.

Chapter Two

Why Integration?

There are 37,034,000 people in the U.S. with physical disabilities — the largest American Minority (U.S. Bureau of the Consensus, 1984–1985).

Figure 1.1: Nearly 20 % of the American Public are considered disabled. (My estimate.)

260 Million people in America

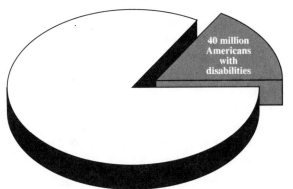

One definition of disability, routinely published by the U.S. Federal Government, states that, "A disabled person is an individual who has an impairment that significantly limits them in one or more daily life activities, or are considered, by themselves or others, to have or to have had such a condition." (Funk, 1986, p.17) According to a study conducted by Lou Harris and Associates, 14 percent of all Americans 16 years of age and over, or 27 million people are disabled. If we add the two million people who are institutionalized and the nine or more million disabled people under 16 years of age, there are close to 40 million persons with disabilities.

Moreover, of the 27 million persons

Figure 1.2: These
numbers will increase as
society ages. (Funk, 1986)

with disabilities in the Harris Poll, 44% have physical disabilities, 13% have sensory impairments; e.g., speech, vision, hearing, language, 6% have mental disabilities and 32% have other health impairments. Overall, findings consistently indicate that persons with disabilities have little opportunity for employment, access to community resources, and/or discretionary income that persons who are able-bodied often enjoy (Funk, 1986).

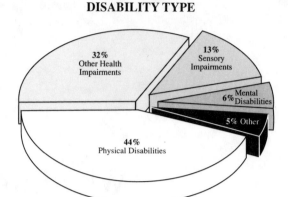

DISABILITY TYPE

As Adventure leaders, it is significant to remember that the vast majority of individuals with disabilities live in the community. However, very few frequent Adventure programs. It is time to be proactive and welcome all citizens into community services — not just physically but with effective social interaction and social acceptance.

Benefits of Integration

There is justification and a place for segregated Adventure programming. In fact, the segregated Adventure programs — those in rehabilitation centers, institutions, special schools, etc., — are thriving. However, the most difficult challenge, where the largest number of individuals with disabilities live and work, exists within the community. For individuals with disabilities, integrated Adventure experiences should be the priority in most cases and segregated experiences considered an alternative or "stepping stone."

It has been recognized that integrating persons with disabilities into community programs can benefit all participants. The inherent benefits of the Adventure experience — especially those of group orientation — fit well with what researchers have already realized; that nondisabled persons benefit from integrated programs (Schleien & Ray, 1988). In fact, it is my opinion that by including persons with different abilities in Adventure programs, facilitators will become more effective leaders. Mainstreaming will challenge the facilitator to be more dynamic in providing curricula for individuals who have a wide continuum of interests and abilities.

More importantly, as participants become more diverse, we will begin to "walk our talk." For example, Adventure education is effective for differently-abled groups because of the principle of "challenge by choice," where participants are allowed to participate on their own level, at their own pace, as determined by themselves. This is a unique philosophy in human services. In addition, common selling points of the Adventure movement have been the focus on the "generalist" nature of the leaders and the flexibility of the curricula. Given these attributes, it is only natural that the Adventure education field serve as a model for integration — one that other professionals can follow.

It is well documented that integration enhances the lives of persons with disabilities via role-modeling by nondisabled peers (Brinker, 1985; Donder & Nietupski, 1981). The many opportunities for individuals with disabilities to enhance their social skills and physical capabilities through Adventure education should not be delayed any longer.

As a therapeutic recreation specialist, I have had many opportunities to work with segregated groups. After a successful year of Adventure programming with young adults who have cerebral palsy, I questioned them as to what additional Adventure activities they would like to participate in (the budget for this program was plentiful). Unanimously, the participants said that they wanted to participate with peers who were nondisabled, regardless of the activity. The participants wanted to socialize with peers who lived in their neighborhoods — not continue to be bused to the segregated programs. This poignant letter supports this example:

Dear Playground Director:

I was told about the playground you want to build for kids like me and regular kids, and that you were looking for ideas from handicapped kids. We really need a place to play, and maybe if I tell you about my normal day in the summer, you will understand.

I lie in bed an hour to an hour-and-a-half after I wake up, while Mom makes breakfast. I can help mom make breakfast. I just don't do it as fast as Mom, and with two brothers and sisters, I 'get in the way.'

After breakfast, I roll out to the sun porch, while Mom cleans the house, or does the laundry, I could help with the cleaning, but Mom can do it faster, and...I 'get in the way.'

Most days, I go outside in the backyard and play by myself, or with our dog. We have a basketball hoop on the garage, and I'm pretty good, especially my hook shot. I know I could play with my brothers and their friends, but I slow down the game, so most days I sit in the backyard reading, or playing with the dog. It seems to me, we are both put out here so we won't be in the way. The only difference is the dog can run off and play with his friends when he wants...I can't...Deep down inside I know I can do just about anything anyone else can do, just a little different, just a little slower. It just seems I don't get a chance very often...or at all.

For a week every summer, I go to camp for special kids. It's fun, but it's only for a week a year, and even when I enjoy playing and winning against another handicapped kid, it would be much better to play and win against a regular kid.

So Mr., I'm sorry I don't know how to spell your name...it's too long, but if you build a playground where I can go anytime and can play with regular kids, and not be in anyone's way, I'll play in it and I'll buy you a 'Big Mac' with cheese and a coke.

I won't sign my name, because it might hurt my family a little, and they do love me, very much so do your best please.

Yours truly,
A friend from Springfield

(From Oestreicher, M. (1990). Accessible Recreation: 20 Years Behind The Times. Parks and Recreation Magazine, August, p. 52–55)

Legislation

Several key legal and legislative actions have led to a new paradigm for serving individuals with disabilities in the community. some of these significant events include:
- Brown v. Topeka, Kansas, Board of Education (1954); ruled that segregation of students by race is unconstitutional. Furthermore, education is a right that must be available to all on equal terms.
- Mills v. Board of Education of the District of Columbia (1972); declared the exclusion of students with disabilities from free, appropriate education, a violation of due process and equal protection clauses of the Fourteenth Amendment to the Constitution.
- Public Law 93-112, Vocational Rehabilitation Act of 1973, Section 504 (1973); states that individuals with disabilities cannot be excluded from participation in, denied benefits of, or subjected to discrimination under any program or activity receiving federal financial assistance.
- Public Law 94-142, Education for all Handicapped Children Act

(1975); provides a new authority extending free and appropriate public education for all children with disabilities, ages three to five, and a new early intervention program for infants and toddlers.

- The Americans With Disabilities Act (ADA) P.L. 101-336 (1990); gives civil rights protection to individuals with disabilities in private sector employment, all public services, public accommodations, transportation and telecommunication.

A Closer Look

More recently, legislation has been passed that will have a direct impact on Adventure programs. Since the Americans With Disabilities Act (1990; known as ADA) will have immediate influence on Adventure and related programs, let us start here.

The Americans With Disabilities Act (ADA) (P.L. 101-336; U.S.C. 12101), signed into law by President Bush on July 26,1990, will affect all citizens of the United States. Built upon existing legislation (Rehabilitation Act of 1973 and Civil Rights Act of 1964), the law provides a clear and comprehensive national mandate for the elimination of discrimination against persons with disabilities.

More specifically, the *Handicapped Requirements Handbook* (1990), reports the objectives of the Act as: a), to provide a clear and comprehensive national mandate for the elimination of discrimination against individuals with disabilities; b), to provide clear, strong, consistent, enforceable standards addressing discrimination against persons with disabilities; c), to ensure that the Federal Government plays a central role in enforcing the standards established in this act on behalf of disabled persons; and d), to invoke the sweep of congressional authority, including the power to enforce the fourteenth amendment and to regulate commerce in order to address the major areas of discrimination faced day-to-day by citizens with disabilities.

With nearly 40,000,000 Americans with a physical and/or mental disability (and the number is growing as the population ages), most Adventure leaders will have at some point in their careers an opportunity to work with such persons. It is my hope that professionals in the field of Adventure education will be proactive and not reactive when it comes to legislation.

In order to determine whether your program and facility fall under the legislative requirements of ADA, you can obtain a copy of the ADA Requirements, along with other timely legislative information, from:

Thompson Publishing Group
1725 K Street N.W. (Suite 200)
Washington, D.C. 20006

See Appendix A: Resource Section for more information on the Americans with Disabilities Act.

In 1973, Public Law 93-112, the Vocational Rehabilitation Act was passed by Congress requiring that federal fund recipients make their programs and activities accessible to persons with disabilities. In 1976, the Department of Health, Education and Welfare issued general standards and procedures to serve as guidelines for all funding agencies (published in 1978). In 1980, President Carter transferred lead agency coordination over to the Justice Department. The regulations were reissued in 1981.

It is important for Adventure leaders to be aware of two major Sections in this law. Section 504, which emphasizes program accessibility; and Section 502, which is concerned exclusively with implementation of architectural standards prescribed in response to the Architectural Barriers Act of 1968.

Section 504 — requires the establishment of an environment in which all persons with disabilities may participate in programs and activities and receive all services, without barriers to full participation.

The regulations included are designed to eliminate discrimination on the basis of disability in programs and activities receiving federal financial assistance. Federal financial assistance is any grant, loan, contract, or any other arrangement by which the agency provides or otherwise makes available assistance in the form of funds, services of federal personnel, or real or personal property.

"Program or activity" includes state or local government agencies and entities that receive funds from such agencies; entire colleges, universities or school systems; corporations or other private organizations that are engaged in providing education, health care, housing, social services, parks and recreation or that receive federal financial assistance as a whole; and any other organization that is established by two or more entities described above.

Section 502 — requires that any facility constructed, leased or altered by the federal government or with the use of federal government funds be accessible to persons who are physically disabled.

Section 502 established the Architectural and Transportation Barriers Compliance Board (A&TBCB) to enforce the prescribed accessible standards. In 1984, four federal agencies developed and published the prescribed accessible standards and called them the Uniform Federal Accessibility Standards (UFAS), now accepted for use under the Architectural Barriers Act of 1968. This Act was

It is clear that all new construction will require accessibility — including ropes/challenge courses (Did you know that companies spending money on access for persons with disabilities can take a deduction of up to $15,000 per year, under changes made to the tax law in 1990? Also, firms with gross receipts under $1 million or with fewer than 30 employees, that spend between $250 and $10,250 on access, may claim a tax credit of as much as 50% of the cost.)

established to insure that certain buildings financed with federal funds are so designed and constructed as to be accessible to persons with physical disabilities. UFAS are also recognized as interim standards for the Americans With Disabilities Act until new standards are developed — these standards are now available and can be obtained through your State Government Agencies.

There are several other laws that Adventure leaders should become aware of, including Public Law 94-142, Education for all Handicapped Children Act (1975). Remember that, with the passage of the Americans With Disabilities Act, all legislation will undergo change, so it is imperative for all leaders to locate a source for ongoing information concerning the legal requirements for accessibility. A good place to start is with your state agencies. Also, refer to Appendix A: Resource Section, in the back of this primer.

GENERAL OVERVIEW OF EXCEPTIONALITY

Most ideology upon which outdoor Adventure programs are based is quite holistic in perspective, and emphasizes the importance of recognizing and accepting the individuality of *all* persons (Smith, 1990, p. 212). Every person with a disability has his or her own unique life story to tell...and no label or characterization can give you, as an Adventure leader, a clear indication of the strengths and weaknesses of that individual. You first have to spend time with each person.

So why label? Many professionals point out that labels are necessary for several reasons: a) the funding of social services; b) in assisting us in communicating more effectively (as professionals); and c) in providing a common ground for evaluating research findings (Hardman, et. al., 1990). One "group" that has been dramatically effected by labeling are persons who are mentally retarded. But consider that labeling has been a mixed blessing for these individuals; while it has been the basis for the development and provision of services, it has also promoted stereotyping, discrimination and exclusion (Roos, 1982). Upon reading the general overview that follows, remember that: "...the categorizations involved are seldom behaviorally or diagnostically exclusive or inclusive. Not all members of any given group possess all of the characteristics noted for that group,

and most of the members of any group possess some of the behavioral characteristics of other groups" (Smith, 1990 p. 212).

Keeping this in mind, Section Two is intended to provide readers with
information regarding general characteristics of individuals with certain disabilities and explores such categories as mental challenges, behavior challenges,
physical challenges, health challenges, and visual and hearing impairments.
Areas such as learning disabilities, attention deficit disorders, multiple disabilities and others were not included due to the limitations of a primer. Adventure
professionals should pursue additional knowledge and skills relative to providing experiences for persons exhibiting a broad range of abilities, and continually
reflect on their personal competence required for diverse programming.

Chapter Three

Mental Challenges

I t is estimated that between one and three percent of the total American population are mentally retarded (Haring & McCormick, Eds., 1990). Some causes of this disability have been identified as infection; e.g. rubella, trauma; e.g., injury during birth, nutritional; e.g., thyroid dysfunction, gross postnatal brain disease; e.g., tuberous sclerosis, unknown conditions; e.g., hydrocephalus, chromosomal abnormality; e.g., Down Syndrome, gestational disorders; e.g., prematurity, psychiatric disorders and environmental influences; e.g., sensory deprivation.

Grossman (1983), is given credit for the most widely accepted definition of mental retardation. This definition, favored by the American Association on Mental Deficiency (AAMD), reads:

Mental retardation is defined as significant subaverage general intellectual functioning resulting in or associated with concurrent impairments in adaptive behavior and manifested during the developmental period.

In order to more clearly understand this definition, consider the following labels, classifications and definitions.

Intelligence

Upon referral by a teacher or psychologist, a person is given an I.Q. test. This score is compared to the average I.Q. (100). If the score deviates significantly (Below 70; Haring & McCormick, Eds., 1990), then the person may be considered mentally retarded. A further classification would include the severity of the condition such as mild mental retardation if the I.Q. is between 55 and 70, moderate if 40-55, severe if 25-40 and profoundly mentally retarded if the I.Q. is 25 or lower. According to Hardman et al. (1990), general characteristics might include:

Persons who are mentally retarded can participate in many Adventure experiences, regardless of their label.

Educable (55-70)
Functions on a second to fifth grade academic level and will be able to adjust, socially, with a fairly high degree of independence in the community.

Trainable (40-55)
Primary focus is on self-help skills with limited academics; may work in a supervised work and living situation.

Severe/Profound (below 40)

May not be able to take care of basic needs. A significant level of care and supervision will be required during the individual's lifetime.

Adaptive Behavior

In addition to a standardized I.Q. test, persons identified as mentally retarded may be evaluated on their adaptive behavior. This includes the person's ability to meet standards of maturation, learning, personal independence and social responsibility that would be expected of another individual of comparable age level and cultural group. More specifically, can the person cope with the demands of his or her immediate environment? Specific adaptive behavior scales are used for assessment purposes.

Developmental Period

In order to differentiate people who are diagnosed as mentally retarded from those who have been brain injured or have had a stroke, the developmental period refers to the period of time between birth and eighteen years of age.

Many children and adults who are mentally retarded are being mainstreamed into society. It is likely that the Adventure leader will have an opportunity to provide programs, both segregated and integrated, for these individuals. The Adventure professional is encouraged to pursue additional information and training with persons who have mental challenges.

Some Suggestions for a Successful Adventure Experience

- Keep the directions for the Adventure activity concrete; avoid abstract concepts.
- Use contact with the equipment and/or elements; e.g., ropes course, versus representation as much as possible.
- When sequencing the Adventure curricula, allow more time during transition stages/periods.
- Allow for the continued "practice" of social skills when engaged in the Adventure program; e.g., being part of the group, proper language, waiting their turn to participate.
- Make sure the person(s) under-

The majority of individuals who are considered mentally retarded are labeled mildly mentally retarded.

Allow for concrete methods, such as drawings, to process the Adventure experience with persons who have mental challenges.

stands the directions for the activity and has an opportunity to express ideas, fears, confusion, etc.

- Allow for concrete methods to draw conclusions from the experiences; e.g., picture drawing as a method of debriefing.
- Make sure there is adequate time for each element to avoid undue pressure (See Appendix C: Safety Considerations).
- In planning the Adventure sequence, allow for a broad range of gross and fine motor skills.
- Stress the concept of "challenge by choice" (see Appendix D: Key Definitions and Terms).

Behavior Disorders

Behavior is a relative term. As society embraces a wider continuum of behavioral expression, we may see less of a need to label individuals as being mentally ill or having an abnormal personality. According to Smith (1990), outdoor Adventure programs have been offered to three subgroups of persons with behavior disorders, including:

Persons with serious personality and adjustment disorders
Historically considered "psychotic," this group includes schizophrenia, childhood dysfunctions of schizophrenia, symbiotic psychosis and early infantile *autism. The individuals in this sub-group typically require hospitalization and have received Adventure curricula in therapeutic forms.

Persons who are "neurotic"
These people make up the majority of persons who have been considered as behaviorally disordered. Typically, these individuals may have a problem of ego strength, self-concept and poor social adjustment. Although some of these individuals require hospitalization, the

majority are served in special educational settings and community mental health outpatient programs.

An additional subgroup
Usually children who experience emotional distress, which is often recognized as a result of transient or situational stress. Trauma such as physical or sexual abuse, parental divorce, poor academic performance, death of grandparents and other situational stress can require a "working through" of the difficulties. Adventure programming has lent itself to addressing these issues with both children and adults.

Note: There is some evidence that autism may be of organic etiology. Some characteristics of persons who are autistic include: avoidance of others, disinterested in receiving affection, exhibits oddly repetitive behavior; e.g., rocking, self-inflicted aggression and may repeat sounds or what is said (Heward & Orlansky, 1988).

There is little agreement in the literature on the definition of behavior disorders. However, the Federal Register offers the most supported definition in terms of funding for school-age children. It includes the following description and characteristics for the term *Seriously emotionally disturbed.*

1. The term means a condition exhibiting one or more of the following characteristics over a long period of time and to a marked degree, which adversely affects educational performance:
    a. An inability to learn which cannot be explained by intellectual, sensory or health factors;
    b. An inability to build or maintain satisfactory relationships with peers and teachers;
    c. Inappropriate types of behavior or feelings under normal circumstances;
    d. A general pervasive mood of unhappiness or depression; or
    e. A tendency to develop physical symptoms or fears associated with personal or school problems.
2. The term includes children who are schizophrenic (or autistic). The term does not include children who are socially maladjusted, unless it is determined that they are seriously disturbed. (U.S. Department of Health, Education and Welfare, 1977, 42, No. 163, p. 42478)

There are a number of Adventure programs that serve individuals who are considered having behavior disorders. Most Adventure leaders have had to confront and process behavior problems. *Islands of Healing*, (1988) offers an extensive model for implementing Adventure education programs with persons who have behavior challenges.

The following suggestions may prove helpful in enhancing an Adventure program which is accessible to individuals with behavior problems:

- Acquaint yourself with the categories and subcategories of the American Psychiatric Association Diagnostic and Statistical Manual of Mental Disorders (DSM-III & DSM-III-R).
- Provide a carefully structured Adventure curriculum; if there are to be unstructured activities, clearly distinguish them from structured activities in terms of time, place and expectations.

- Let participants know what you expect of them and how much assistance you will provide.
- Reinforce appropriate behavior.
- Model appropriate behavior and refrain from words or actions you do not wish to have participants imitate.
- Plan for gradual change during the Adventure program.
- Vary the presentation format of the Adventure curriculum; e.g., combine group instruction, experiential learning, independent exercises and other teaching practices in the program.
- Be fair and consistent. However, it is safe to temper your consistency with flexibility.
- Balance individual needs with group requirements.
- Be aware of the many nonverbal cues that are important for understanding the needs of the participant (See Appendix C: Safety Considerations).
- Be prepared to receive acts of anger and aggression without reciprocating; view disruptive behavior as expressions of past conflict; do not be confused with approving of or condoning disturbed behavior.

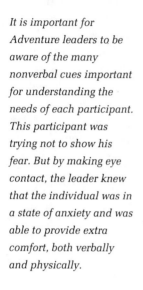

It is important for Adventure leaders to be aware of the many nonverbal cues important for understanding the needs of each participant. This participant was trying not to show his fear. But by making eye contact, the leader knew that the individual was in a state of anxiety and was able to provide extra comfort, both verbally and physically.

Chapter Four

Physical Challenges

The majority of persons with physical disabilities live in the community — approximately 95%. However, this particular group is difficult to classify due to the number of conditions, as well as the fact that some individuals also have related disabilities; e.g., communication, speech, vision and hearing.

A common definition used to describe orthopedic impairments will add clarity to this chapter. According to the Federal Register (1977), orthopedic impairments are disabilities that relate to the skeleton, joints, and muscles, including: a) the absence of some member of the body or other congenital anomalies; b) impairments caused by diseases; e.g., poliomyelitis; c) impairments caused by cerebral palsy; d) amputations; and e) contractures caused by fractures or burns. The causes of physical disabilities can be as varied as the disabilities themselves, including:

Prenatal — before birth. Causes can be genetic, which are transmitted from the parents to the child. An example would be Muscular Dystrophy — a sex-linked recessive gene transmitted through unaffected mothers to their sons. Also, causes can be a result of external influences such as a fall by the mother during pregnancy and inadequate prenatal medical care.

Perinatal — first labor pain to infant's first breath. Injury can result from insufficient oxygen to the child, an example would include strangulation by the umbilical cord.

Postnatal — birth to two years. Typically, disabilities can result from car or bicycle accidents or from diseases — bacterial and viral infections that attack the central nervous system (Haring & McCormick, Eds., 1990).

It would be impossible to review all of the characteristics and types of physical disabilities with which the Adventure leader may come in contact. However, it is important to consider some of the realities related to physical disabilities. There is some agreement that the age of onset has an influence on how individuals with disabilities adjust to their impairment; for example, for persons born with a disability (congenital) they do not know what it is like to walk and may adjust gradually; e.g., if they are born unable to progress to ambulation, they will never know what it was like to walk. However, if they are injured later in life they must deal with both their pre- and post-accident functioning. Remember though, each person has his or her own history. Whether a person is disabled at birth or later on, his situation is unique and cannot be generalized. Each person deals with her disability in her own unique way. Adventure leaders should receive the participant with the disability as they do anyone else, with a clean slate, without assumptions.

Additional factors that influence the impact of physical disability include: the degree of disability; visibility of condition; e.g., how a person adjusts to public reaction; family and social support; attitudes toward the individual; e.g., expectations by leaders; social status with peers; e.g., a narrow definition of beauty by society can add pressure, architectural and transportation barriers.

Let us take a closer look at some of the more prevalent physical disabilities.

Cerebral Palsy

Cerebral palsy has been described as a neurological syndrome that is caused by damage to the motor control centers of the brain. Approximately half of the individuals with cerebral palsy (1.5 to 5 per 1,000 births) have "normal" intelligence. (It has been my experience that more than half have normal intelligence, and since I haven't been able to define what is "normal intelligence," I assume that until proven otherwise, the person understands everything I'm saying.) This condition can occur before, during or after birth. According to Kirk (1989), there are three major types:

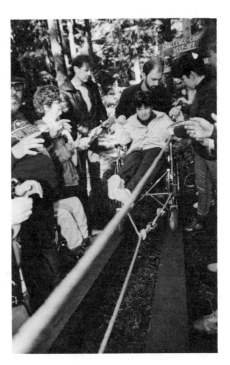

Adventure education experiences offer opportunities for individuals with cerebral palsy to move in new ways.

Spastic cerebral palsy
Muscle tone is abnormally high (hypertonia) and increases during activity. Both muscles and joints are tight or stiff, and movements are limited in affected areas of the body.

Athetoid cerebral palsy
Muscle tone is constantly changing, usually from near normal to high. Movements are uncoordinated, uncontrolled, and jerky.

Ataxic cerebral palsy
The child with this form of cerebral palsy has severe problems with balance and coordination (usually ambulatory).
(p. 501)

Individuals with cerebral palsy can have one or a combination of the three major types of conditions — along with learning disabilities, mental retardation, seizures, speech problems, eating problems, etc. Moreover, the affected areas can include one side of the body (hemiplegic), either legs or arms (diplegic), or the whole body (quadriplegic).

Muscular Dystrophy

Adventure activities can be made accessible for persons with Muscular Dystrophy.

Muscular dystrophy is considered an inherited condition which is musculoskeletal in nature — the muscles weaken and deteriorate. There are a variety of types with the cause attributed to heredity (although not confirmed). Specific cases — Duchenne Type — can lead to an early death, with individu-

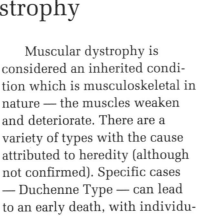

als losing the ability to walk in early adolescence. The loss of mobility is the result of fatty tissue gradually replacing muscle tissue. Approximately 200,000 people are affected by muscular dystrophies and other neuromuscular disorders. It is important for Adventure leaders to understand that the majority of persons with muscular dystrophy have a "normal intelligence — otherwise, their disability usually does not affect their intellectual ability." Also, these individuals tire easily, and those who are ambulatory may be prone to falling, causing injury or frustration. Many use either manual or electric wheelchairs for mobility.

Spina Bifida

Spina Bifida is a condition which occurs before birth. The nervous system is affected — for some reason (unknown) the backbone of the developing fetus remains open. Spina Bifida may or may not influence intelligence but frequently involves some form of paralysis, depending on the location of the defect in the spinal column (See Figure 2.1). According to Hardman, et al. (1990), there are two major types:

Spina Bifida Occulta
A very mild condition in which a small split is present in one or several of the vertebral structures. Many people are not aware of the problem until they have an X-ray. There are typically no related abnormalities or functional problems.

It is helpful to have mats available in order to make the Adventure experience more comfortable for the participant who has Spina Bifida.

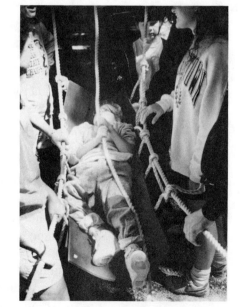

Spina Bifida Cystica
(Two types): *Meningocele*, a tumorlike sac on the back of the infant containing spinal fluid but no nerve tissue, and *Myelomeningocle*, a sac which does contain nerve tissue. This condition can cause partial or complete paralysis of certain body areas, lack of bowel and bladder control and mental retardation (I have not experienced many people with Spina

Bifida as having any intellectual problems or mental retardation — so I was surprised that this information existed in the literature. Once again, it is my advice to never assume that a person with a physical disability also has intellectual barriers).

Spinal Cord Injuries

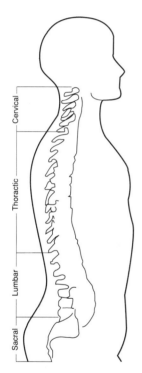

Injury to the spinal cord is usually a result of trauma caused by diving, automobile, or motorcycle accidents. The cord can be traumatized or severed. The majority of spinal cord injuries happen to males during their 20's. As many as 500,000 people are living with spinal cord injuries (Maddox, 1990). In order to comprehend the impact of the spinal cord injury, it is important to understand the spinal column. There are 33 vertebrae — 7 cervical (in the neck area); 12 thoracic (in the chest area); 5 lumbar (in the back area); 5 sacral (fused, in the lower back area); and 3, 4, or 5 coccygeal (fused, in the tailbone area).

Immediately following an injury to the spinal cord, it is difficult to assess the damage until the swelling subsides. However, the individual may end up with one of the following conditions:

Quadriplegia
All four extremities are paralyzed. Complete interruption of the ascending and descending tracts below the level of the injury (usually in one of the 7 cervical area vertebrae).

Quadriparesis
All four extremities are weakened rather than paralyzed. There is damage to the area (one of the seven cervical vertebrae) but some of the sensory and/or motor fibers below the lesion are intact — also known as incomplete paralysis.

Paraplegia
Includes lower-extremity paralysis. Complete interruption below the level of injury (usually below the cervical vertebrae, in the thoracic, lumbar, sacral, or coccygeal regions).

Paraparesis
Lower-extremity weakness. (Hanak & Scott, 1983)

The individual who has a spinal cord injury, as well as his or her family, confronts a variety of issues following the rehabilitation process. These issues may include cardiovascular considerations,

Figure 2.1: In order to understand the impact of the spinal cord injury, it is important to understand the spinal column.

respiratory problems, nutritional concerns, urological implications, gastrointestinal management, skin care, musculoskeletal effects, sexual functioning and the many psychological "processes" involved in moving ahead. Adventure education programs have been gaining acceptance in the rehabilitation community as outlined in this newspaper article from the *Salt Lake Tribune* (May 8, 1989):

Camp Teaches Handicapped to Reach Inside, Take Calculated Risks and Build Confidence

By Mike Gorrell, Tribune Staff Writer

In the three months since he was paralyzed, Kent Harris has learned a lot about himself.

He discovered a little more Tuesday in the blooming hills above Camp Kostopulos in Emigration Canyon.

Bob Dunn isn't physically disabled. But he, too, recognized a valuable lesson during a session on the camp's new "Accessible Adventure Challenge Course."

The course is basically a mixture of ropes and wooden beams that could blend into the scenery at any Army boot camp.

One stop along the way is called the "Burma Bridge." An inverted pyramid of attached ropes — one on the bottom to walk along, two up top to hold onto, and a half dozen or so linking top to bottom — it looks like the kind of bridge Indiana Jones would use to cross a deep river gorge to avoid becoming a headhunter's dinner in some steamy jungle.

At another stop, there's a beam that could challenge the balance of any gymnast.

And at a third, there's a series of ropes hanging from a horizontal beam, all several feet apart. The idea is to grab the first rope, get it swinging back and forth so you can grab the next rope. Then repeat the process until you reach the beam's other end.

It's tough work.

But that is the purpose, said Dr. Mark Havens, a special education instructor who developed the course.

It challenges everyone who tries it. It makes people reach down inside and find a way to do something they might not have thought was possible. It doesn't matter how. Just as long as they do it.

"It's primarily (designed) to help people learn to take calculated risks, to develop self confidence, " said Dr. Havens, who founded Accessible Adventures as a company to help disabled children and adults gain access to challenging experiences in education, recreation and the outdoors.

Kent Harris has faced plenty of challenging experiences since Jan. 10, when his lower back was broken by a patio cover that fell under a heavy load of snow.

"I'm pretty new at it still," he said Tuesday, shortly after he'd tested himself on a configuration of ropes that resembled an upside-down Burma Bridge. Lying on his back, he pulled himself along a rope from one side of the apparatus to the other.

The experience, the 28-year-old Ogdenite said, was a "big boost to my confidence." And, as he noted, overcoming the mental and emotional hardships associated with a disability are tougher than dealing with the physical difficulties.

"No matter what anybody tells you, that's the hardest part," he said. "You have to learn how to handle things. A lot of it's fear. I have extra fears to deal with now... I'm getting over it slowly. I have no choice. I have to. It's not a question of if you're coping it's how well you are."

"Precisely," Dr. Havens said.

In many cases the disabled have been overprotected from real life by well-intentioned parents and therapists. They've been funnelled into programmed activities where they don't learn to take risks. Consequently, when real life poses a real challenge, some aren't prepared, either physically or mentally.

Through the challenge course, Dr. Havens said, "they get a chance to be involved. They're idea of what's normal widens. They can realize they're not disabled. They just move differently. Other people just move differently. That's important."

The course stimulates creativity since there are no rules on the best way to do things. It builds muscles. It builds confidence. It can make participants more willing to tackle tasks that seemed frightening beforehand.

Hanak & Scott (1983), provide general guidelines for potential functioning levels (musculoskeletal) for individuals who have spinal cord injuries. It should be noted, however, that there are many other emotional and physical factors that influence each person's functional capabilities. The "golden rule" in this section is to remember that each individual brings with him different abilities and support systems. While these classifications are important for awareness purposes, they offer little guidance as to how an individual will function in Adventure programs:

Injured Area (See Figure 2.1)

C-4

This person will need a motorized wheelchair; can be independent in operating wheelchair (mouthstick), writing, typing, and in performing a variety of electronically-initiated activities. Person requires a personal-care attendant. Has use of scapular muscles and diaphragm.

C-5

May have use of deltoids, partial biceps and some scapular muscles. With orthotic devices, can perform light grooming, communication activities and feed self. Can participate in some sports with accessible equipment.

C-6

Has use of biceps and wrist extensors. May be able to transfer self, care for personal needs, drive a car, and participate in accessible sports/activities.

C-7/8

Has shoulder muscles and triceps. This person may be totally independent in personal-care activities.

T-1/5

Has use of all of the above muscles plus hand and intercostals (some). Uses wheelchair, however, is independent in all activities. Can transfer from chair onto floor and participate in a variety of movement activities.

T-6/12

The additional muscles innervated at these levels include intercostals and abdominals. The individual will have better balance, enhanced respiratory abilities, and will need less energy to perform self-care activities. May ambulate with long leg braces.

Many individuals with spinal cord injuries are participating in Adventure experiences.

L-1/3

Muscles innervated at these levels include the iliopsoas and the hip adductors. Individuals with these injury levels may ambulate with short leg braces.

L4-S2

Muscles innervated at these levels include the hamstrings. Some ankle and foot musculature also will be present. Individuals with these injury levels may ambulate with minimal aids.

Regardless of the injury, most Adventure experiences can be made accessible with persons who are physically disabled. Ask them for suggestions — they are the experts!

Amputations

There are approximately five amputations per 1,000 people in the United States (Hardman, et al. 1990). These individuals are usually injured or have some type of bone cancer. In addition, children can be born (congenital) with amputations. The fetus — reason unknown — either does not fully develop a limb or is lacking the entire hand or foot. It is generally agreed that children born with amputations generally have an easier time adjusting to the treatment and therapies required for adjustment. The individual who receives an amputation later in life may experience shock, denial, and other adjustment problems. Once again, it has been my experience that each individual reacts to his injury differently. I know people whose amputations occurred late in life, and who are adjusting very well. And I know individuals who were born with an amputation, who constantly struggle with accepting their situation — so, each situation, and each individual is unique.

Persons with amputations are involved in a variety of outdoor pursuits, including adventure, challenge experiences.

Persons who have injuries resulting in amputation, go through the following:

- Medical Care: The physician prepares the remainder of the arm or leg for eventual use with a prosthetic device.
- Coping Strategy: Involves processing the feelings and self-perception that emerge as a result of the loss of a limb or limbs.
- Rehabilitation: An interdisciplinary team of health professionals work together with persons who have had amputations to assist them in adjusting to their condition and prosthetic device. (See Appendix D: Key Definitions and Terms.)

There have been many breakthroughs in the development of prosthetic devices, which are now more comfortable and effective. It is important for the Adventure leader to challenge participants with amputations to perform at a rate commensurate with their abilities — which may assist in the adjustment to the amputation.

Arthritis

It is important to encourage warm-up sessions prior to initiating Adventure activities; this is a general guideline, regardless of the ability level of participants.

Juvenile rheumatoid arthritis affects people in their early years. The condition can affect the entire body and cause respiratory infection. Prior to joint pain and swelling, the child may experience fever, rash, lung fibrosis and eye pain. The child can have remission, the cause of which is unknown. Typically, more females acquire rheumatoid arthritis, with close to 200,000 children being affected (Hardman, et al. 1990).

Approximately one percent of the adult population can have some form of arthritis, experiencing pain in and around the joints. Early diagnosis is important and Adventure programmers should note that persons experiencing any form of arthritis should be encouraged to be as independent as possible. However, warm-up activities are necessary (especially in the morning) and participants should be encouraged to move around frequently.

Epilepsy

Some programs require individuals with seizure problems to wear helmets on the ropes course. In this case, it may be wise to require all participants to have helmets — this way, the person with seizure problems is not singled out.

Abnormal or excessive electrical brain function causes seizures which may or may not be associated with other physical problems; e.g., cerebral palsy. According to Hardman, et al. (1990), there are two major types:

Tonic/clonic

Formerly known as *grand mal*, individuals may experience a unique sound, odor, or physical sensation just prior to the seizure. Person loses consciousness and falls to the ground; this is the tonic phase. The trunk

and head become rigid. This rigidity is followed by violent shaking — the clonic phase of the seizure. The participant may experience irregular breathing, blueness of the lips, increased salivation, loss of bladder/bowel control and perspiration. Some seizures of this type can last 20 minutes (see Appendix C: Safety Considerations for suggestions on how to assist with a seizure).

Absence

Formerly known as *petit mal*, individuals may appear in daydream-like state — characterized by moments of inattention and accompanied by rapid eye blinking or head twitching. These seizures can occur over 100 times a day for some individuals.

The cause of seizure disorders is not widely understood. The prevalence of this condition fluctuates as well. It is likely that Adventure leaders will have to handle a seizure at some time in their career. There is a tremendous amount of stigma attached to individuals with seizure disorders and the professional is encouraged to practice confidentiality. The Adventure leader's reaction to a seizure serves as a powerful model.

Multiple Sclerosis

Multiple sclerosis (MS), affects nearly 500,000 people (between the ages of 20-40) in the United States. It is a chronic disease and is experienced by more women than men. The cause is still unknown. MS attacks the myelin sheath, which is the coating around the nerve fibers in the brain and spinal cord (See Figure 2.1). Where the myelin sheath is attacked and destroyed, it is replaced by plaques of hardened tissue — at first, the nerve impulses in the area are interrupted, then can be obstructed all together. This leads to (depending on the area attacked) blurred vision, numbness or tingling in the hands, slurred speech, staggering gait, and tremors. Eventually, there may be paralysis.

People with MS can experience remissions where the symptoms disappear. However, this is only temporary and the condition reappears, which can obviously be frustrating. The person with MS is encouraged to be as active as possible. The Adventure leader is encouraged to program in "rest periods" when programming with persons who have MS. The Adventure experience can be exciting for individuals with MS. However, make sure you take the time to work with the person in setting goals for participation.

Conclusion

It is almost impossible for any professional to be aware of all the characteristics and implications present in working with individuals with physical disabilities. The Adventure leader is encouraged to network and consult with others to accommodate persons with all physical abilities. The following suggestions may enhance the successful inclusion of people who are physically disabled in Adventure curricula:

- Assume until proven otherwise that persons with unintelligible speech understand on a higher level than their expression indicates.
- Ask the person with a physical disability what adaptations, special equipment, or teaching procedure would work best for her.
- Consult with experts on safety precautions (particularly if the participant is a child).
- As much as possible, allow the participant the opportunity to do what peers do; even though her disability may cause her to appear uncoordinated.
- Openly discuss uncertainties on when and how to assist an individual.
- Help others understand and be aware of such things as drooling and physical awkwardness; e.g., no ridicule. The Full Value Contract, in *Islands of Healing*, (1988), is a significant resource for use with diverse groups. (For example, if the group contracts not to ridicule one another, there is then a guideline for dealing with such behavior if and when it occurs.)
- As much as possible, treat the individual with a physical disability like everyone else; promote risk-taking, don't overprotect, etc.

Chapter Five

Health and Sensory Challenges

"The most important thing to remember about chronic illness is that it is exactly that — chronic — it never goes away." (Robert Massey, age 29 who has hemophilia; Patterson, 1988.)

These are some of the health disorders with which the Adventure leader may come in contact with over the next several years — Heart Disease, Cystic Fibrosis, Sickle Cell Anemia, Cancer, Acquired Immune Deficiency Syndrome (AIDS), etc. It is advised that the leader consult the primary expert — the person with the condition. There are also allied health professionals who are eager to assist outdoor leaders.

I recommend that Adventure leaders acquaint themselves with a Physician's Desk Reference for clear definitions of health disorders. (An example is: Barnhart, E.R. (1991). *Physicians Desk Reference*, 45th Edition, Oradell, NJ: Medical Economics Co., Inc.) There are some simple, practical things to remember to ensure that the Adventure experience is a positive one for persons with health and sensory challenges.

Some Tips to Remember
- People with chronic conditions (especially children) may be limited in the types and number of different experiences that are appropriate for them to participate in.
- Some of these conditions are not visible and must be identified carefully through non-threatening means.
- A child should learn to explain her disability, respond to questions and know when to ask for and decline the help of others.
- The stress of the Adventure experience, particularly the fear reaction to high elements, can effect the individual with a medical condition. Careful screening and monotoring of these individuals, and close cooperation with specialists is recommended.
- Effective health forms should be a requirement for any Adventure program. Allow time to talk with individuals, who have health challenges, prior to the activities.

A couple of specific conditions that Adventure leaders can expect to address and should be aware of are:

Diabetes

Diabetes is a metabolic disorder characterized by the inability of the body to use sugars and starches. Consider that glucose (a sugar), which is one of the end products of digesting carbohydrates, is used by the body for energy. Some is used right away; the rest is stored. However, muscle and liver cells cannot absorb and store the glucose (energy) without insulin, a hormone. Insulin assists the body by allowing the glucose to enter the body's cells. Without insulin, the glucose accumulates in the blood.

Prior to the discovery of insulin, Hyperglycemia (increased concentrations of glucose in the blood), caused many individuals with this condition to experience diabetic ketoacidosis — symptoms of which include extreme hunger, thirst and a need to urinate (can result in a coma). Added complications, if not treated, can include blindness, cardiovascular disease and kidney problems. Juvenile diabetes can be particularly challenging and tends to be more severe. Adults develop the problem in their 40's and usually can monitor the condition independently. It is important not to generalize — everyone deals with his or her condition differently.

Adventure leaders need to be aware of this condition, particularly with children (peak incidence periods for children occur around 12 years of age). Appropriate foods should be made available and logistics should be worked out so the participant has an opportunity to monitor and adjust his insulin. Also, in some cases hypoglycemia can develop (caused by too much insulin, exercise, etc.). Symptoms include irritability, poor attention span, temper tantrums and weakness.

Asthma

Asthma is characterized by difficulty in breathing — excessive coughing, wheezing and a build up of phlegm. The degree of severity varies with each individual who has the condition. With both children and adults, there seems to be a strong relationship between psychological well-being and the presence of asthmatic conditions. This is important for Adventure leaders to remember as stress may trigger periods of asthma for those who have the condition.

Moreover, the facilitator of Adventure curricula should be aware of the embarrassment a person may have after an attack of asthma. Proper screening and communication with all participants will alleviate these situations.

Visual Impairments

"Taking risks is necessary for everyone because security is mostly a superstition. Life is either a daring adventure or it is nothing."
(Helen Keller)

A legally blind person is said to be one who has visual acuity (keenness) of 20/200 or less in the better eye even with the aid of glasses or whose field of vision is narrowed — the widest diameter of her visual field subtends an angular distance no greater than 20 degrees (field of vision narrows). More specifically, Seaman and DePauw (1989) provide the following classification of visual impairments:

Levels of Impairment

Legal Blindness (20/200)
The ability to see at 20 feet what the normal eye can see at 200 feet.

Travel Vision (5/200 to 10/200)
The ability to see at 5 to 10 feet what the normal eye can see at 200 feet.

Motion Perception (3/200 to 5/200)
The ability to see at 3 to 5 feet what the normal eye can see at 200 feet. This ability is limited almost entirely to motion.

Light Perception (less than 3/200)
The ability to distinguish a strong light at a less than distance of 3 feet from the eye what the normal eye would see at 200 feet. Motion of the hand at 3 feet would be undetected.

Total Blindness
The inability to recognize or respond to a strong light shone directly into the eye.

Only about 20 percent of the people considered blind are totally without sight. In an educational setting, there is a distinction between persons who are blind and those who are partially sighted — this is done in order to determine the level and extent of additional support services required. As an Adventure leader you may come in contact with persons who have the following functional abilities:

Persons with total blindness can participate in a variety of outdoor experiences. Adventure curricula helps individuals who are blind make the transition to outdoor experiences which can enhance their lifestyle.

Profound: performance of the most gross visual task may be very difficult; vision is not used at all for detailed tasks.

Severe: more time and energy are needed to perform visual tasks; performance level may be less accurate than that of sighted individuals even though visual aids and modifications may be in use.

Moderate: visual tasks may be performed with the use of special aids and lighting; performance level may be comparable to that of sighted participants.

According to many textbooks, an individual who is blind at birth has more barriers to overcome than those who become visually impaired later in life. I have found this to be relative to the individual. Related problems some individuals encounter when they are blind include learning problems, perceptual motor development, speech and language skills, and social development. The following suggestions may assist Adventure leaders in accommodating individuals who are blind:

- Structure the Adventure environment so that the participant who is visually impaired can anticipate activities and the physical layout.
- If a blackboard or overhead projector are used for instruction, make sure you verbalize the written materials.
- Present materials and/or activities in a hands-on, manipulatable manner rather than in an abstract format.

Hearing Impairments

"My feelings aren't mine alone. I feel they reflect the overall resentment the deaf community has towards mainstreaming. The trend in education today is to integrate (another term for mainstreaming) students with diversified backgrounds, races, and abilities. Deaf students are guinea pigs in a national experiment being conducted in laboratories (read: schools) across the country ." — Bahan *(In the* Network News, *Boston University, 1990, p. 4)*

This is a good point to make the statement that all professionals and participants are not in favor of mainstreaming — particularly those who are deaf and/or blind. However, the Adventure leader should have a basic understanding of persons who are hearing impaired and be aware that integration is still an issue. But, it is important to be aware that there is a deaf community and I encourage all persons to learn sign language which will allow you to communicate with and understand persons who are hearing impaired. (I recently conducted a teambuilding program at a junior college for 36 freshman who are deaf. These participants made it clear that they preferred to be called "Deaf," not hearing impaired. Hearing impaired implies a problem, and they informed me that they have their own culture and

language and do not consider themselves having a problem or impairment.)

Deafness is considered a hearing impairment so severe that the person is impaired in processing linguistic information through hearing, with or without amplification, which adversely affects learning performance. A hard-of-hearing person is one who, with the use of a hearing aid, can process some linguistic information through audition (the act of hearing). The age of onset is critical in determining the type and extent of intervention a person receives. Classification of the severity is outlined by Hardman, et al. (1990) as follows:

Insignificant: no real difficulty with faint or normal speech.

Mild: frequent difficulty with faint sounds; some difficulty with normal speech (conversations).

It is a necessity to have interpreters for Adventure programs which integrate persons who are deaf.

Moderate: frequent difficulty with normal speech (conversations) and loud speech.

Severe: frequent difficulty with even loud speech; may have trouble understanding shouted or amplified speech.

Profound: usually cannot understand even amplified speech.

There are a number of Adventure programs underway for individuals who are deaf. Many exist, however, at residential schools; e.g., Gallaudet, and the Southwest Collegiate Institute for the Deaf of Howard College. As mentioned before, the prevalence of mainstreaming individuals who are deaf is still an ongoing debate. It is important, however, to consider the following suggestions for programming with individuals who are deaf or hard-of-hearing:
- Allow the participant with a hearing impairment to be where he can easily see your lip movements.
- Do not speak too loudly, especially if the participant is wearing a hearing aid.

- Avoid wearing jewelry or other apparel that may be a visual distraction.
- Avoid standing with your back to the person and moving around while giving directions.
- Work with the participant and her interpreter for the best arrangement on the challenge course for effective communication.
- Always provide written instructions to go along with verbal information.

A Final Note

Adventure professionals should pursue additional knowledge and skills relative to providing experiences with persons who have a broad range of abilities. Continually reflect on your level personal competence required for diverse programming. Consider this experience:

I accepted the challenge of using a high ropes course with children who had diabetes. I figured that, as a therapeutic recreation specialist, I had the necessary training to safely accommodate this group of students. What I had not realized was that the activity - high ropes elements - had an impact on the students metabolism; e.g., even while waiting to climb, the students were under stress and their blood-sugar levels were taxed). During the activity, several students had problems related to their diabetic conditions. I should have been prepared to address this situation; e.g., by monitoring blood-sugar levels at all times, having snacks at the site, using a more sequential approach to the high elements). The experience ended as a success and there were no injuries, however, a better understanding of diabetes by myself would have made this experience safer and more effective for all persons involved.

This experience sheds light on the gray area of integration and mainstreaming. Where is that line between the necessity for specialized programming/training and simple access to existing adventure programs?

As more people with disabilities are integrated, into existing adventure programs, the answer will become more clear. Some professionals in educational programs have found that it is unfair to the students with disabilities, the able-bodied students and teachers when integration takes place without proper training and orientation.

This section deserves some concluding comments. Knowing how much to include or whether to include any information at all on exceptionality in a primer is a difficult decision. In order to successfully integrate persons with disabilities in community Adventure programs, a great deal of cooperation among community Adventure leaders, specialists and persons with disabilities will be required. The community Adventure leader will have to be motivated to learn about and spend time with persons who are disabled. The specialist will have to be willing to counsel, educate and cooperate with the community leader. And, the person with a disability will have to willingly serve as a resource and leader as he or she participates. My intention for including this section in the primer is to stimulate awareness among community Adventure leaders and provide a beginning point for understanding diversity. All the facts and figures provided are meaningless without interaction among diverse groups of people. I encourage the reader to reach out both experientially and intellectually in order to better prepare for integrating his or her programs.

Section Three

BUILDING BRIDGES

Any major change begins with the individual. This section encourages adventure leaders to address their own level of comfort with respect to working with persons who are disabled. The fact is that integration is hard work. Read the story by Project Adventure trainers Lisa Furlong and Carey Yeo. Put yourself in their place when leading a group which feels that the person with the disability is holding back the group's progress. How do you answer their concerns while taking care of the feelings of the person with the disability? How do you sensitize the group to *want* to include all persons in all activities — the heart of Adventure programs?

These are tough questions that Adventure leaders increasingly will be faced with. But as Adventure leaders, we cannot expect others to welcome the integration of all persons until we ourselves are able to answer these questions and expand our own comfort levels.

Chapter Six

Starting With Yourself

With important legal and legislative history in place and general support for integration, why are so many people with disabilities absent from community activities — including Adventure programs? An answer to this question would require a text in itself. However, in my opinion, it is apparent that our society has a certain "comfort" level in terms of what is "normal" physical, intellectual and behavioral functioning. Consider this example:

There is a story told about an educator who has tremendous success placing individuals with severe disabilities in work settings. He had an individual with Autism working effectively on an assembly line — in fact, this worker was one of the top assemblers. However, the worker sat in the lunch room during his break and rocked back and forth — perhaps a behavior learned while institutionalized. This behavior bothered his co-workers (obviously challenging their comfort levels). There was considerable discussion among the administrators about dismissing this individual, even though his work habits were outstanding. The professor, being quite creative, developed a strategy with the worker. During the break times, the worker wore headphones, which appeared to be attached to a radio in his pocket. It now looked as though his rocking was due to a common behavior — keeping time with the music ("rocking out"). This behavior was acceptable to his co-workers and fit nicely within their continuum of what is appropriate behavior. As a result, this individual kept his job at the factory!

Whether or not this was an appropriate remedy for the situation is not the point of this story. It simply speaks to my observation that perhaps the single most significant barrier to overcome with regard to integration and/or accessibility is "attitudinal." *Integration can be hard work!* It will require all of us to reflect on the social conditioning we have received concerning what is, according to "our mind's eye," comfortable and acceptable.

Personal Reflection

My own attitude about working with people with disabilities has changed considerably over the years. My early training was founded on a clinical/medical model. I received a great feeling of self-worth and a sense of "power" when programming for persons with disabilities. Diagnosing someones' weaknesses, planning activities to remediate them, and determining whether there is progress can provide a sense of importance to a professional — most people want to be considered an "expert" at something. However, I have found that this "model" of helping is incomplete. For persons with disabilities and the people who work with them, a new paradigm is necessary. Both the professional helper and the person with a disability require a different relationship with one another. Some assumptions I have about making this interaction a reality include:

1. Professionals and participants need to come together as co-learners in the use of Adventure curricula.
2. Diversity in each group should be celebrated as an opportunity to learn, not a problem to be solved.
3. "Specialists" need to work cooperatively with community professionals and participants in order to make the transition from segregated to integrated programs.
4. All Adventure leaders, regardless of their specialty, need to expose themselves to more diverse groups including age, cultural backgrounds, abilities, etc.
5. Each participant we work "with" should be appreciated for her unique set of abilities, interests and limitations; e.g., her humanness.

The move toward integration will not be easy. There will be a great deal of resistance from parents of persons who are disabled (they have been disappointed many times from unkept promises), professionals who may feel threatened by giving up their power as "experts," individuals with disabilities who may not feel comfortable in integrated settings, community members who are uncomfortable around persons with disabilities, etc. However, Adventure education is all about taking risks and celebrating diversity — a strong philosophy which give us, as Adventure leaders, an excellent place to begin this process of making Adventure learning accessible.

A Reflective Story

Lisa Furlong and Carey Yeo, Project Adventure Trainers, recently experienced integration at work during an Adventure Based Counseling Workshop. Their story exemplifies both the power and struggle of integrating Adventure curricula.

Growing Through Experience

by Lisa Furlong and Carey Yeo

How Loretto House and the Iron Rail (PA's Hamilton, MA training facilities) could be accessed by a person in a wheel chair was possibly the most ringing question on peoples' minds on first hearing that one of the participants in a recent ABC workshop was spinal cord injured and required the use of a wheelchair for mobility. As we embarked on this new area of training, however, the questions of physical accessibility soon became the easy ones.

Having Ann as a member of the group gave added dimension to the issues of diversity that ordinarily arise during an ABC workshop. What became increasingly clear as the days progressed was that accessibility has a lot more to it than ramps in appropriate places. Accessibility is truly, as Mark writes, an attitude. Throughout the five-day workshop, we were constantly challenged to create an atmosphere of accessibility which met both the physical and emotional needs of a very diverse group of people.

Ann recognized that there might be limitations to what she could and could not do but was always willing to try new activities, acknowledging that a participant in a wheelchair was new for us here at PA. The learning that took place for us and our workshop group over five days was tremendous. So, we felt that we'd like to share our interpretation of the *what*, the *so what* and the *now what* from this experience.

What?

About a week before the workshop, we got a phone call from Ann, inquiring about the accessibility of our buildings. We let Ann know that it was not great but

By using the expertise available, Adventure leaders can improvise when adapting safety/tie-in systems for high elements. The safety and comfort of the participant, however, remain the highest priorities.

that we would do whatever we could to help her stay. As the week progressed, the problems with the buildings became glaringly clear. In a number of ways it was a frustrating week for Ann — having to rely on many of us to help her with the Loretto House stairs, not being able to get lunch at the Iron Rail, not having an accessible bathroom on one floor at Loretto, etc. The list could go on and on. We are sure that all of us are aware of the problems; but are we aware of the emotional toll these obstacles can take on a person over the course of an already strenuous workshop? Think about having to ask for help every time you needed to go to the bathroom.

On a more positive side, the actual workshop experience was a positive, yet hard one, for all of us. We were able to make a variety of physical adaptations on the course that worked quite well. What we soon found was that some of our assumptions about Ann's potential level of participation were not quite accurate. Another learning from Mark that worked — when in doubt, ask. Ann was willing to experiment with our ideas and had a lot of good ones of her own.

Making it a partnership for learning helped to make all of us more comfortable. Below is a list of some of the challenges that we encountered and changes that we implemented:

Games

- On day one we were headed outside to the lower grassed area at the front of Loretto House to start the intro warm-up and name games — Ann via the back way, the remaining group out the front doors (there are even steps *outside* at Loretto House). Ann reported that the lawn was not too bad to move across but a little tough for playing tag games.
- A walking pace in the tag games worked okay, and things seemed pretty even, that is, until we played hospital tag; one tag and Ann could only turn circles! Ann was left stationary when playing Hog Call, moving forward and bumpers up being an impossible dual feat. The other games we played that morning, Toss a Name, Speed Rabbit, Impulse, came off with no hitches.
- The morning warm-ups at the Iron Rail were soon shifted from the grassy area to the paved roadway and the area in front of the barn doors....much to Ann's relief. We all soon found that grass and wheel chairs do not mesh.
- We were continually challenging our assumptions about what games could and couldn't work. Turnstile turned out to be a particularly emotional group problem solving effort.

Trust Sequence
- **Two Person Fall** — During the afternoon of the first day, we

worked through a trust sequence. When it came to the one and two person trust fall, Ann was able to tell us where her center of balance was and suggested the best place for fallers to stand so they could be safely caught. A person's center of gravity will vary according to the type of injury that has necessitated the use of a wheelchair.

- **Trust Circle/Levitation** — The circle pass was out (for Ann as a participant, not as a spotter) for obvious reasons. The levitation worked quite easily, however. Ann was able to lock her leg braces, and her back brace kept her back straight.

- **Fall from a Height** — Since Ann works largely with disabled clients, she was eager to have the group experiment with a number of ideas on how to safely complete a trust fall. Ann had previously done a fall from a held standing position (level of lesion and use of calipers enabling this). On this day Ann chose to fall from a sitting position. Spotting was the same as for a usual Trust Fall except that her head and lower back were caught. Spotters ensured that Ann's legs didn't hit or scrape the platform that she was falling from. She suggested that the area beneath the butt and legs be padded since some people may have particularly fragile skin.

Initiatives

- Ann took an active role in almost all of the Initiatives. Two that were particularly unaccessible were the Wild Woozey and the Criss Cross. Any activities on the cables were a problem.

High Course

- **Flying Squirrel** — we used a Troll sit harness plus chest harness with a front clip-in. At Charlie William's (PA builder) suggestion, Ann was pushed toward the group as they were running back. This gave plenty of time for the wheelchair to be taken away and there was still a big swing to be had.

- **Belay School** — using a sticht plate, Ann found that the energy required to both hold herself upright in her chair, and belay a little difficult. By

Often some well thought-out technical adaptions to safety attachments enable a person who uses a wheelchair to partici-pate fully in the Adventure experience—even the Flying Squirrel!

holding her upper body to the back of her chair with webbing, Ann found the action of belaying and holding a falling climber a relatively easy task. On stationary climbs, Ann was parallel to the climber (facing him or her), with the back up belayer at her side and her back-up holding the back of her wheel-chair. On traversing climbs, Ann was positioned with her side to the climber, back-up belayer behind her, and her back-up either pushing the chair forward when the climber was traversing, or holding the chair down from the side when the climber was climbing, stationary or being lowered. On lowering climbers from the various elements throughout the fourth day, the wheelchair had no tendency to tip.

Sometimes the greatest obstacle to a person who uses a wheelchair is not the element itself, but rather the attitudes of others. This participant spent two hours making her way to the top of the Vertical Playpen.

- **Vertical Playpen** — This was the major element that Ann climbed. She reached the top after two long hours, climbing with two different partners. Based on her experience, Ann recommended that there be removeable parts on the climbing elements. This way we would not have to build separate adaptive elements, but could provide for varying abilities on one element.

So What?

Creating ropes course elements and games that were accessible for Ann seems to have been the easy part. We had a great deal of help from Bob Ryan and Charlie Williams in making us comfortable with and knowledgeable about technical pieces. Ann certainly did her share in helping to develop comfortable adaptations for the high and low course. The *so what* about what we did seems to center around the questions and issues that arose around emotional accessibility.

The group progressed tremendously over the course of the workshop, but on day one the expectations and assumptions were often surprising. During the trust sequence, Ann shared that she had some experience with ropes course work, but that she was still experimenting and was interested in having the group experiment with her. She was very open and honest about knowing her own physical limits and wanting the group to feel safe with her. Following a brief discussion, we moved onto the Two Person Trust Fall. Not one person was willing to fall into Ann's arms, even after we both gave it a very safe go.

As we progressed through the trust sequence, people seemed to relax a little around Ann and the Levitation was quite comfortable. The Trust Fall seemed to bring people a little closer together, with Ann looking for ideas about how other people with disabilities might be able to fall. In the evening session, with the sharing of goals, we were able to get out into the open what seemed to have been the elephant in the living room. Several people were concerned that by being in the group with Ann, they would be slowed down.

This very interesting session led us to begin to think about the accessibility of the model and the role of the facilitator in setting expectations. The reality was that certain adaptations were going to have to be made — a very significant one being that the pace needed to be slower than we might normally expect in a five-day workshop — lunches and breaks needed to be longer; travel time between elements took longer; and generally, the amount of running needed to be curbed. All of this seemed to have a real impact on the group with some people feeling like their physical expectations of the workshop were not being met. While many questions arose from this, one of the most important was "how could we address these issues without Ann becoming the *sore thumb* of the group?" Should we, as facilitators, push the issue, or should we wait for the group to make it their own issue?

It was clear to both of us that we had opinions about how *we* thought the group should deal with the issues at hand. What was also clear was that our ideas were not necessarily meshing with those of the group. What arose, which is typical of all workshops, was a delicate balance between what we thought should happen and how the group chose to do it. What we found that was not so typical was our own level of emotional investment in the group's choices. We were clearly affected by our own needs for the group to be responding the way we thought they should be, which was not necessarily the way they were!

The overriding theme of the "so what" for both of us is that, as we begin work in adapting our courses for accessibility, the true effort must be in creating climates that embrace and honor differences in a ways that do not make the differences stand out. This task is much more complicated and delicate than either one of us could ever have known before this workshop.

Now What?

There are still many unanswered questions for both of us about what we could have done differently and even more about how PA is going to go about making its workshops accessible to everyone. We do not think these questions are going to be easily answered, but we are both committed to pursuing issues around adaptability. We are both excited for the potential learning and changes that PA can make. We look forward to the challenge ahead.

Reflective Practice

This timely story brings to the forefront many questions and processes the Adventure leader will have to address in the move to accessible Adventure programs. I invite you to reflect on the following questions gleaned from the story:

1. Are you willing to consider that accessibility should be a priority for Adventure leaders and programs?
2. Are you willing to advocate for the inclusion of persons with disibilities in your programs and others? Are you willing to deal with accessibility at your site — raising necessary funds and convincing others that it is important?
3. Are you willing to expand your own comfort level in terms of appreciating differentness?
4. Are you willing to be aware of how your language reflects your attitude? Are you willing to explore whether you are willing to accept a wide continuum of intellectual, behavioral and physical ability?
5. Are you willing to address the emotional, intellectual and physical issues — interpersonally — that arise when you are around persons with disabilities?

These questions and many others get to the heart of the matter. If we are to see successful integration in the 1990's, people have to address the feeling side of mainstreaming. The physical adaptations and the technical knowledge will be the easy part of the move to diversity in Adventure programming. In order to move towards providing social interaction and acceptance of persons with disabilities in our Adventure programs, we also have to address our own social conditioning and prejudices.

Awareness Raising

"Words are the basic units of speech by which we communicate ideas and thoughts." (Deloach and Greer, 1981)

The selection of language reveals to others our perception of the world and ultimately influences and constructs how others perceive us. When a person uses slang or pejorative terms in reference to persons with disabilities, listeners become aware that the speaker is unaware of acceptable language. For example, many people use the term "cripple" to refer to a person with a physical disability. According to the Oxford English Dictionary, the term "cripple" means "to creep," which connotes an image of a person crawling or dragging himself along. A more acceptable description would be to emphasize the person first and then the physical disability; e.g., a person with a physical disability.

It is not uncommon for Adventure program facilitators to use the term "handicaps" when describing persons who experience a variety of physical or emotional disabilities when participating in an activity. When assigning role playing activities, many facilitators select terms such as "mute" or "cripple" to describe an individual's role. It is important for Adventure leaders to understand the etymology of certain words so as to not be pejorative or insulting while facilitating experiential curricula. Moreover, the terms or language that facilitators use during training sessions is often mimicked by the participants, creating an opportunity for modeling sensitivity in language and avoiding an acceptance of using "unacceptable" language in both professional and personal settings.

The use of unacceptable jargon is further reinforced by mass media reports that are imitated by the general public. Such terms construct negative images of persons with disabilities and indirectly illicit patronization or feelings of pity among the audience. The audience should be cognizant that "slang" terminology simply reflects the speaker's personal point of view and how he imagines he would feel under similar circumstances. The expressed fear of being born or becoming disabled serves to perpetuate attitudinal barriers to integration of abled-bodied and disabled persons in Adventure programs. Let us take a closer look.

Suggestions for Using Appropriate Language

Language you should not use.
These words have strong negative connotations because they tend to focus on what a person cannot do.

Preferred language.
These words are more affirmative and can reflect a positive attitude by focusing on each individual as a person first.

Avoid	Suggested
handicapped/handicap	person with a disability
cripple, crippled by	individual with a disability
victim	person with multiple sclerosis (MS)
spastic	person with cerebral palsy (CP)
patient (except in hospital), invalid	person who had polio

stricken with "___" .... person who has muscular dystrophy
suffers from "___" .... person with an emotional disability
crazy, manic, insane, retard, retardate,
idiot, imbecile, feeble-minded .... person with an intellectual disability

Avoid	Suggested
birth defect, inflicted .... caused by "____"	
afflicted/afflicted by	
incapacitated, poor, unfortunate .... born with "____"	

Avoid	Suggested
wheelchair bound .... mobility impaired	
confined to a wheelchair .... wheelchair user	

Avoid	Suggested
the blind .... visually impaired	
sightless .... sight disability	
deaf and dumb, deaf-mute .... deaf, hearing impaired	
the deaf .... hearing disability	

Avoid	Suggested
normal, regular person .... nondisabled	

(Adapted from **Focus on Abilities**, 1988; available from the Ability Center, Toledo, OH)

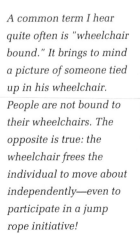

A common term I hear quite often is "wheelchair bound." It brings to mind a picture of someone tied up in his wheelchair. People are not bound to their wheelchairs. The opposite is true: the wheelchair frees the individual to move about independently—even to participate in a jump rope initiative!

The Adventure facilitator has a tremendous potential to interact with a wide continuum of professionals and participants. The opportunity to "model" appropriate attitudes through language is a beginning step towards successful integration of Adventure experiences.

Challenging Comfort Level

It is important for Adventure leaders to challenge their own comfort level while programming with persons who are disabled. The obvious and most effective way is by associating with individuals who are disabled. Deloach and Greer, (1981) suggest the following guidelines for effective communication with individuals who are disabled:

"Do not be overly sensitive regarding the inappropriateness of everyday expressions."
As a facilitator, do not be afraid of "slipping" or using everyday expressions when talking with a person who has a disability; e.g., when talking with a person who is blind, don't worry if you say, "See what I mean?" Persons with disabilities, as with all of us, often intuit whether someone is being insensitive. In fact, if you are comfortable with everyday language around persons with disabilities it may be complimentary.

"Be aware of what terms are 'in,' as well as what terms are considered antiquated or demeaning by the disabled, but be very cautious when using them."
As with any group that has shared common experiences, persons with disabilities sometimes use words such as "gimp" to communicate with each other or build unity. Moreover, a person with a disability may use "A.B." to describe an able-bodied person. It becomes the responsibility of the Adventure facilitator to find out the "in" terminology and keep up with the changes in her local area. However, use caution!

"Be extremely careful in using reference to 'normal' people."
People with disabilities do lead normal lives. To refer to oneself as "normal" negates the status of any person who may have a physical, emotional or intellectual disability. It is more acceptable to use "nondisabled," "temporarily able-bodied (a TAB)," or even a "walkie." Our definition of what is "normal" in society is very narrow. Adventure curricula is based on concepts that allow for a wide continuum of ways to solve problems, play, interact and take risks. Let's live the model!

"Attempt to stay away from 'zoo keeper' phraseology."
People with disabilities are not impressed when able-bodied persons use such phrases as, "A good friend of mine who is deaf...," or, "My mom teaches the mentally retarded." When such phrases are used it can be taken as an attempt to document the speakers knowledge of a subject based on social aquaintence. It may not be possible to understand another person's life without asking questions and getting to really know one another — the essence of adventure.

Bloom County; BLOOM COUNTY by Berke Breathed. (c) Washington Post Writers Group. Reprinted with permission.

"Don't be afraid to admit ignorance on a topic or subject when it seems necessary to understand the gist of a conversation."
Adventure facilitators will often be perceived as being more sincere and "real" if they are honest and open about their lack of knowledge concerning disability. Too often, the persons with disabilities are on the "taking" end of interactions. Solicit their expertise and both parties will learn.

"When in doubt, use everyday language."
When in doubt, use simple language. Nothing is more discrediting than using incorrect technical terminology. Do the best you can to stay current. Specialized fields are constantly revising and changing terms. Professionals in the fields of Special Education and Rehabilitation have a difficult time staying current. The following article from the **Oregonian**, Wednesday, August 29, 1990, demonstrates the ongoing debate on language use:

New Word for Disabled Could Be Worth $50,000

By M.L. Elrick (Knight-Ridder Tribune News)

What's in a word? Maybe $50,000. That's the prize offered by the New York-based National Cristina Foundation, which is sponsoring a contest to create a new, positive word to describe disabled people and "raise awareness of the fact that there are a group of people in our society who have not been sufficiently recognized for their abilities, " says Yvette Marrin, president of the foundation.

Marrin, an educator who holds a doctorate in organizational administrative studies and special education, says terms such as, "disabled," "handicapped" and "crippled" have negative connotations that affect people's attitudes about those with disabilities.

"Your perception of a person is sort of shaped by what is the terminology used to describe them, " she says. "The mind-set of society needs a new word."

Finalists, selected by the English department of Johns Hopkins University in Baltimore, will be judged by a panel of well-known novelists, journalists, etymologists and people with disabilities.

Marrin, who does not have a handicap, lists the National Council on Disability, the Council for Exceptional Children and National Rehabilitation Association as supporters of the contest.

But some disabled Detroiters feel the contest is misguided.

Sue Latcha, a former board member of the Easter Seal Society of Wayne County, Mich., says she doesn't mind terms like "disabled," "handicapped" or "physically challenged." "I don't really care, as long as you don't refer to me as 'crippled,' or I'll smack you, " says Latcha, who has cerebral palsy.

She does, however, care about the $50,000 being offered by the National Christina Foundation.

"Fifty thousand dollars is a nice incentive to come up with a new word, but to me it's not important. People are going to call me whatever comes to mind anyway, " says Latcha, who works as a volunteer in the Education Resources For Students with Disabilities office at Wayne State University in Detroit.

"We don't need a new word," she says. "We need education."

Chet Simpson, program director of the Health Education Association and member of the Michigan Organization for Human Rights, agrees. He believes the contest's prize money could be better used.

He says he's concerned that another word might further confuse the public. He would prefer to see the money spent on advertising or promotions to get people to work more closely with the "physically challenged." That term — along with "handicapped" and "disabled" — seems fine to him.

Entries should be either a new word or new combination of existing words. Entries must be postmarked by Nov. 30 and sent to: NCF Contest, 2301 Argonne Drive, Baltimore, MD 21218.

More than one entry per person is allowed, but only one entry per postcard or letter. For more information, call (900) 988-WORD. There is a $3 charge for each call.

A Personal Response

While my Aunt was critiquing this primer, she was affronted by this article. She wrote the following in response to a new "word" for the disabled: "Why a 'catch-all' identity? I am Shirley Michel. I have been a child, a wife, a parent, a grandparent, a senior citizen, etc. I have experienced childhood, marriage, grandparenthood, widowhood, and aging. I am none of these transitory descriptions — I am Shirley Michel. I am shaped by my experiences but they have not changed my identity — old or young, fruitful or barren, married or widowed — Who am I? I am Shirley Michel."

Using Simulations

A word of caution about the use of simulations. A definition for simulation from the **New World Dictionary**, Second Edition (1978), is; "to have or take on the external appearance of; look or act like (an insect simulating a twig)" (p.1328). Simulations of disabilities are common practice and can be effective – some popular exercises include: using blindfolds, cotton in the ears, non-speaking roles, spend a day in a wheelchair, etc. However, it is important to explain to participants that, while they may know and experience what it is like to have a blindfold on for a time, they do not know how a person who is blind feels. It is kind of like "an insect imitating a twig."

Consider this article, excerpted from the **SCS Newsletter**, 1990. Scott Balko is the Wisconsin coordinator for the Spinal Cord Society. In response to employees of a hospital in his hometown "playing handicapped person for a day," he wrote the following:

Let's Play Disabled for a Day

by Scott Balko

I would like to make a few suggestions for these adventurous people next time they decide to play their little game...experience being paralyzed for one year. And during this year do the following: get a bedsore — get one that won't heal, so that you have to get plastic surgery; experience some urinary tract problems; choose whichever problem you wish, infection, stones, dysreflexia, reflux, etc. Or how about some drastic calcium deposits? And let's not forget to throw in a little osteoporosis and some muscle atrophy for good measure...continue on and experience some respiratory problems, like pneumonia. Experience cardiovascular problems. Now go on and experience having your urinary collection apparatus come off and guess what is all over yourself? Do this in a public place.

And then experience an involuntary bowel movement in a public place.

After you have experienced all this, you should experience not liking being paralyzed (this does not have to mean that you hate life. I need to clarify this fact). Therefore you should lobby, fundraise, etc. for a cure. You can listen to them (your therapists, nurses and doctors) tell you to abandon (your) 'false hopes' and that you should accept your paralysis and be happy that, 'after all there isn't anything you could do before that you cannot do now.'

...I suggest you all quit your child's play." (In *Spinal Network*, p. 221)

Simulations can be effective in the use of Adventure education... however, handle with care!

My intention for including this excerpt was to draw attention to the "power" of using simulations. They are powerful enough to help people and they are powerful enough to hurt people and misinform them; e.g., you do not know what it is like to be blind after wearing a blindfold for an hour). Their use, as a powerful learning tool, should always be treated as such. I might add that this excerpt may contain philosophical opinions concerning rehabilitation that some may agree with or disagree. Supporting opinions was not the reason for its inclusion. In my opinion, the excerpt exemplifies the importance of using simulations with care!

In order to raise awareness among staff and/or colleagues, there are sample resources for training in Appendix E.

Chapter Seven

Applying Accessible Adventure Curriculum

Many persons with disabilities do not need adapted equipment or specialized techniques for their inclusion in Adventure programs. As I've stated before in this primer, the major barrier to integrated programming is "attitudinal" — the comfort level of the professional may not be adequate to successfully include persons with disabilities and the person who is disabled may not feel ready for the challenge. The reader is encouraged to spend ample time reading the contents prior to this section. I hope that the tendency to want to get at the "how-to" (integrate) will not take precedence over the "why" (integrate). There is, however, a need for equipment, structures and facilitation strategies in order to assist Adventure leaders in offering

Many professional Adventure leaders may not feel comfortable with persons who have disabilities — this can inhibit them from offering experiences which are integrated.

challenging experiences to participants who have a wide variety of abilities.

The contents of this chapter are not intended to be a step-by-step process on how to include persons with disabilities in Adventure curricula. Rather, the intent is to focus on what is possible. Adventure curricula is inherently meaningful for people of *all* abilities. An excellent rationale for the inclusion of people with disabilities can be addressed by listing the learning goals found in *Cowstails and Cobras II*, (1989):

The child or adult with a disability may not have been exposed to many challenging experiences — this can lead to a hesitancy in signing up for integrated Adventure programs.

1. To increase the participant's sense of personal confidence.
2. To increase mutual support within a group.
3. To develop an increased level of agility and physical coordination.
4. To develop an increased joy in one's physical self and in being with others.
5. To develop an increased familiarity and identification with the natural world.

These learning goals would be supported by many special education and rehabilitation professionals. In fact, similar goals and objectives are present in individual education plans (IEP) and treatment plans for persons with disabilities. Let us take a closer look at curriculum which can be made accessible for persons with all abilities.

Goal Setting

Adventure programs often use individual and group goal setting as a process which can be identified early in the experience, monitored continuously, evaluated and celebrated. This process is invaluable in any growth experience and enhances the participants' ability to set realistic goals for themselves — perhaps leading to a sense of control and responsibility in their lives. Persons with disabilities, particularly children, can be excluded from practicing this process, leading to a sense of dependence on

To develop an increased joy in one's physical self and being with others — This would be a common goal in many special education and rehabilitation programs.

family members and professionals.

Recent attempts in the special education and rehabilitation programs have helped with advocating for the inclusion of students and clients in establishing their own Individual Education Plans and Treatment Plan Objectives. However, more often than not, participants are not active in these important goal-setting experiences.

Islands of Healing, Schoel, et al., (1988) offers some effective goal-setting guidelines. Consider the following suggestions in assuring that persons with disabilities participate in this process:

Conceivable

Conceptualize the goal and make it understandable. You may have to sequence this process for participants with intellectual challenges; e.g., show the participants pictures of the activity and make sure they pictures of the activity and make sure they understand what their choices are. Have them watch others and then make a decision. For non-verbal participants, allow them to "draw" (journal) their goals and discuss their choices.

Always include the participant with a disability in individual and group goal-setting activities.

Believable

The goal must be believable. You need to carefully monitor this one, or participants may set themselves up for substantial failure. (Recognize also that understandable or manageable failure can be beneficial.) Setting realistic goals is a skill and must be practiced. If individuals with disabilities have been excluded from goal setting, particularly children, they may be prone to establishing goals that are out of reach or, on the other hand, feel they can't do anything. Through practice in taking risks and being around good role models, this range in goal-setting will become more balanced and realistic for the child or adult with a disability. Remember, do not make assumptions about what is realistic for individuals who are disabled based solely on what you have read or heard.

Controllable

What factors might make the goal beyond your reach (the things you have no control over)? For individuals with disabilities it may be important to emphasize the difference between "real" and "perceived" barriers. Persons who use wheelchairs for mobility may not be aware of the many options available to them in outdoor Adventure education. Having staff who are disabled is important. They can serve as

Having staff with disabilities provides an opportunity for all participants to experience what is possible.

positive role models and act as a resource for everyone.

Measurable

You need to have some means of reporting back to yourself whether or not you accomplished your goal. Allow individuals with a disability time to reflect on their performance. If they have intellectual challenges, a journal or drawing can be an effective tool for self report. Too often, it is the therapist or educator evaluating "his" performance — we all need to learn to evaluate our own behavior.

Desirable

Your goal should be something you really want to do. This can include things that you have decided to do because they are necessary, though you are reluctant. The "really want to do" goals should, on balance, relate more to what you personally want than to a duty/obligation matrix. Some individuals with disabilities may have difficulty deciding what it is they want to accomplish. It is not surprising, since many of their experiences have been offered in the clinical/medical model setting where activities and experiences can often be prescribed. Choices are important — all participants must know they have them.

Stated with no alternative

Set one goal at a time, without a bail-out plan. If you qualify your goal, there's a tendency to go easy on yourself. An unequivocally stated goal helps keep things clear and uncompromised. But remember too that a goal can be changed at any time. If participants with disabilities have communication barriers, make sure there are alternative methods available to reassess goals and make sure that you as the facilitator are in a position to have eye contact with the participant.

Growth Facilitating

Goals should be positive, so that you can build on them in a healthy way. Negative goals have no place in this process. All participants should be encouraged to set goals that can be built upon — remember, however, that this is a "process" that needs to be made accessible and practiced by everyone.

Activities

The following Adventure activities come from selected materials that are used by facilitators in the Adventure field. Sample activities, from recognized curricula, are followed by suggestions for making the experience more accessible to individuals with disabilities. These suggestions should be used with care.

As mentioned earlier, the general foundation for the activity selection in this primer comes from *Islands of Healing*. There are many methods and opinions for sequencing Adventure activities. The activities chosen for this chapter do not suggest a sequence for programming with persons who are disabled or integrated groups. Rather, they are highlighted to stimulate an understanding of how activities can be made accessible. When integration becomes a reality in the Adventure field, there will be more guidance and models from which to draw. (See Appendix C: Safety Considerations, for more information on this topic.)

Ice-Breaker Activities

"To provide opportunities for group members to get to know each other and begin to feel comfortable with each other through activities, initiatives and games that are primarily fun, non-threatening and group based." (Schoel, et al. 1989, p. 280)

Comfortable Position

p. 41, *Cowstails and Cobras II*

First kneel — keep up a running patter about how important it is to follow your lead exactly — then incline your body slowly forward to a push-up position. Then, even more slowly, continue down to a prone position on the ground. Keep babbling, it's your only smoke screen at this juncture. Lay one hand on top of the other on the ground, point your toes, put your chin on your hands, and smilingly announce THIS is the *Comfortable Position*.

The Comfortable Position!

Toward Accessibility

If you have participants who are mentally retarded, your instructions should be slow and clear. Modeling is the best practice; a leader may be positioned next to the person with a disability.

If a person uses a wheelchair for mobility, encourage her to join the group on the ground (ensolite pads are good to have around for support). It is

It is important to encourage children to get out of their wheelchairs and enjoy the sensory wonders.

helpful to get young children out of their wheelchairs...experiencing the sensory wonders of the ground. Make sure you ask both children and adults if they are comfortable leaving their chairs.

If the person has trouble following the movements of the group, direct each person to get in the comfortable position using his or her own unique movement. This will encourage individual creativity and may take the pressure off the participant who has a disability.

Hey, it works with all people — as the pictures below indicate.

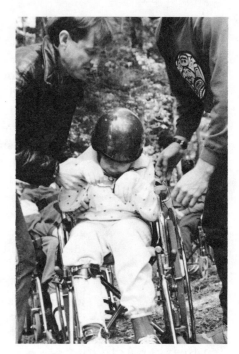

Human Camera

p. 177, *Silver Bullets*

...After having made appropriate comments about how a camera is like a human eye, ask your partner to close his/her eyes, and then lead the partner to a spot where there is an interesting object that you would like to record on retinal film. Using the human camera body as an infinitely mobile tripod, set up your partner's head (the camera) in such a way that his/her closed eyes are directly in front of the chosen subject. Gently pull the ear lobe to activate the shutter. At this encouragement, the "camera" opens and closes the eyelids (shutter) very quickly in order to record the scene. Lead your partner to a few more photographic possibilities and then talk about what you two have jointly recorded.

Toward Accessibility

If your partner uses a wheelchair, you should ask him if he minds getting out of his chair (remember, he has his eyes closed). Be careful to do this activity in an accessible area and, if possible, use a hard surfaced area. It is always easier for participants who use a wheelchair to be on a hard surface so they can move independently.

If a person is visually impaired, she can have her hand be the camera. A quick touch and she has taken her picture.

The Human Camera can be accessible.

De-Inhibitor Activities

> *"To provide a setting wherein group participants are able to take some risks as well as make improvement in commitment and a willingness to appear inept in front of others." (Schoel, et al. 1990, p. 282)*

Inch Worm

p.169, *The Bottomless Bag*

Sit on the turf facing your partner. Inch toward one another until you, and he or she, are close enough to sit on each other's feet. Grasp your partner's upper arm with each hand.

Now, decide which direction you two would like to travel. Lateral movement is out, so it's either north or south. After deciding, the partner (in whose direction you're headed) lifts his/her derriere off the ground and moves a foot or so toward whatever goal you have in mind: be reasonable. The second partner now lifts off the ground and in a cooperative, bug-like movement duplicates the step above and moves toward his/her partner. Attempt to keep your bottom on your partner's feet and help the action by both pulling with the arms and slightly lifting the feet Coordinate your movements and eventually speed up the process so that your pair is indistinguishable from a Loctan herodipus, inching comfortably along a branch.

Toward Accessibility

If one partner has a spinal cord injury, it is important not to sit on her feet (the circulation is restricted already and she will not have much feeling, if any, in that region). However, if you and your partner don't mind, you can get a little closer, with her legs around your waist, and off you go! You may not look like a Locton herodipus, but who cares!

If the person has a cognitive problem, break the activity down into small steps (See Task Analysis, P.?).

Group Juggling

p. 112, *Silver Bullets*

Ask your large group to break up into smaller groups of 5–7. Meanwhile, have available enough comparatively soft, throwable objects — nerf balls, softies, bean bags, tennis balls.— so that there are a few more than one per person. Have the group stand in a circle facing one another, so that the circle's diameter is no more than 12–15 feet. One person in a group of 6 keeps the throwable objects nearby and lobs the ball to a person across the circle. That person lobs the ball to a person opposite from him/her and this continues until a person-to-person sequence is set. Do not throw to the person next to you.

Once everybody knows whom to throw to and receive from, the initiator starts the ball again, but this time includes another ball and eventually

Group Juggling — allowing a pass won't hurt the flow of the activity.

another until there are six balls being kept aloft simultaneously. Try reversing the sequence; i.e., throwing to the person you formerly received from.

Toward Accessibility

If a person with a disability does not have the arm strength to throw, you may have to allow him to pass it to the person next to him. Here is an interesting consideration when making these activities accessible — the question is; should everyone pass the ball to a person next to them so as not to single out the person with a disability? Is it possible to do the activity this way? This is a question that is often asked. To me, the goal of making these activities accessible is to find solutions which do not single people out. However, in some cases it may not be possible to accomplish this goal. I don't have the answers yet, but I am optimistic that as more integrated groups evolve, the answers will come.

For a person with an intellectual challenge, you may want to lay a rope down or chalk in arrows to the person she is to throw to and receive from.

Balls with bells in them are available for persons with visual impairments and it is always good practice to have larger balls available for those who need them.

Cooperative Games

Cooperative games are inherently inclusive and accessible. Competitive activities have a place but can often be exclusive. During the course of my career I have observed many elementary physical education programs. Dodgeball is a popular activity in my home state of Oregon. I have noticed that the slowest student — the one who needs gross motor practice — is the first to get knocked out of the game. He then sits and watches the game progress. The most skilled student — who has excellent motor skills — is usually the last to go out of the game. The result: the slow student participates in gross motor development for a minute

Cooperative games are excellent for involving persons with all abilities. Everyone gets a good workout and they are usually inclusive.

or two (sometimes a second or two), while the student with the best gross motor skills plays for twenty minutes and keeps improving her skills.

There are many skills involved in some cooperative activities and games. If you simply start a cooperative game with persons who are mentally retarded, for example, you may find that the activity is not working.

Amoeba Tag

A large area with boundaries is required. The person who is "it" chases group members (approximately 20) within the boundaries. When someone is touched, she grabs hands with the "it" and continue in pursuit. When another is touched, you have three chasing — holding hands. When a fourth is caught, the "its" can break into pairs — two pairs holding hands — or, stay together as a foursome. This continues until all participants are caught.

Toward Accessibility

For persons who have mobility problems, you can make this game accessible by: a) playing on a solid surface so wheelchairs can be easily moved, b) have all participants run "heel-to-toe" so speed is equitable, and c) shorten boundaries for full participation by all.

Task Analysis

This is a good point to introduce the skill of **Task Analysis** (see pp. 76–77). A task analysis is the identification of all the necessary participant responses, or component skills and the sequence in which these responses or skills must occur, for appropriate interactions with the activity (Wuerch & Voeltz, 1982).

Breaking down social and recreation behaviors and motor skills through the use of task analysis may seem tedious to Adventure leaders (Schleien & Ray, 1988). However, it is a process which may allow persons with developmental disabilities, in particular, to participate in integrated Adventure programs. It will also improve the teaching skills of the facilitator. As the Adventure leader, you will begin to understand the content of the skill and be able to tell the participant what he must do, step by step, in order to meet the goal of the activity.

Sample Task Analysis

The Original Activity

Five-a-Side Flatball

p. 64, *Cowstails and Cobras II*

"Deflate a Moon Ball (aka beach ball) to about 66–2/3 maximum to provide the object-of-play."

"Ten players make up the official roster for this fast-moving game with five players arranging themselves on each side as opposing teams. Use the basketball lines near the end of the court that are parallel to one another and about 6' apart to act as boundary designators. The two teams line up facing one another. Team players should be about arm's length away from one another and facing the members of the opposite team. The suggested lateral boundary lines are 20' apart, measured from side to side."

Object

To smack the flattish ball past the opponent's line using only the front or back of an open hand.

Rules

1. Players must stand with their toes on the line while waiting for a playable hit.
2. When the ball approaches, a player may pivot one step forward to smack the ball, but may not make purposeful physical contact with an opposing player.
3. A point is scored if the ball completely crosses the player's line. If the ball sails over that player's reach, no point is scored.
4. Play begins with a back-handed hit of the ball being held by a fellow player (called a backy). When a team scores, the opposite team immediately initiates a backy to begin play again. There are no time-outs.
5. The ball may not be picked up, held or carried.
6. Five consecutive hits of the ball per side is maximum before the ball must be touched by someone on the other team.
7. Kneeling is not allowed — only foot contact with the floor.
8. Penalties are judged and assessed by the players.

Task Analysis Process

Analyze the component skills required for the participant to meet the objective of the game.

Sample Objective

Presented with the activity, *Five-a-Side*, the participant will play continuously, following the rules, for five minutes.

Component Skills

Stand with toes on the boundary line.
Identify boundary line.
Identify teammates.
Pivot one step forward to hit ball.
Stand arm's length from teammates.
Face member of opposite team.

Recognize when ball completely crosses line.

Recognize when ball sails over player's reach.

Initiate back-handed hit of ball (backy).

Recognize when it is time to initiate backy.

Recognize five hits by own team.

Understand after five hits, other team must hit ball.

Recognize rules; no picking up, holding, or carrying ball; no kneeling.

Recognize play is continuous.

Recognize when to call out penalty.

Whew!

Determine the appropriate sequence of the component skills.

Step 1: Identifies teammates.

Step 2: Identifies boundary lines.

Step 3: Stands with toes on the boundary line.

Step 4: Stand's arm's length from teammates.

Step 5: Faces member of opposite team.

Step 6: Repeats rules (can't pick up, carry, or hold ball; can't kneel).

Step 7: Pivots one step forward to hit ball.

Step 8: Recognizes point is scored when ball crosses line.

Step 9: Puts ball in play after point by other team by initiating "backy."

Step 10: Get's ball if it sails by.

Step 11: Does not hit ball if four hits have occurred on own side.

Step 12: Calls out penalty by others.

Step 13: Plays continuously.

Develop Instructional Units

Break the component skills and sequence of performance into instructional units appropriate to participant's skills and attention span.

Examples

Practice identifying boundary line, standing on line appropriately, getting proper distance from teammate, etc.

Practice pivoting foot forward and striking ball. Practice "backy."

Practice reciting rules.

Reference

There are two excellent resources available for learning activity and task analyses. They are:

Schleien, S. & Ray, T. (1988). *Community Recreation and Persons with Disabilities*. Baltimore: Paul H. Brooks Publishing Co.

Wuerch, B. & Voeltz, L. (1982). *Longitudinal Leisure Skills For Severely Handicapped Learners*. Baltimore: Paul H. Brooks Publishing Co.

Try using the task analysis process on this popular game, People To People *— see* The New Games Book *for instructions.*

Trust Activities

"To provide an opportunity for group members to trust their physical and emotional safety with others by attempting a graduated series of activities which involve taking some physical and/or emotional risks." (Schoel, et al. 1990, p. 284)

Willow in the Wind

p. 52, *Cowstails and Cobras II*

Ten to fifteen people stand shoulder to shoulder in a circle with one person (the faller) standing rigid and trusting in the center. Remaining rigid, the center person falls slowly in any direction. Before he/she moves very far off plumb, the circle people redirect the faller's impetus to another arc of the circle. This fall-catch-shove sequence continues in a gentle fashion until it becomes obvious that the center person is relaxing (but remaining rigid) and that the circle people have gained confidence in their ability to work together toward handling the occasional weight shift of the faller.

Toward Accessibility

If the participants are mentally retarded, you can model what "standing rigid" involves; also, if you draw a circle on the ground it, will remind participants to keep their feet together. It is possible to hold the feet if it is okay with the faller. Also, the faller can stand in a cardboard box (with low sides). Start in close and move out, but be aware that some participants may be intimidated by the "closeness." It is possible, in some cases, to have a person fall "with" the participant in the middle. A big bear hug, both participants are rigid, and away you go. There should be adequate spotting however.

People who use wheelchairs can also participate. If you properly spot the wheelchair (you have to know which parts do not come off), they can go for a ride as well (it is easier if you pass the person in an arc — not completely around or he may fall forward; also, it helps to lock the brakes). If the person wants to get out of his chair, you can all get on the ground. Again, a pad is helpful to prevent pressure sores, and an arc (half circle) is best.

Levitation

p. 53, *Cowstails and Cobras II*

But we can all levitate. Not "stripped of the bonds of earthly ties," but making full use of a friendly group's hands-on offer of fleeting zero G's. More succinctly, having a group slowly lift your prone bod from the ground, to a well overhead position, is a dandy way to build trust and feel good. Just get lots of people to kneel around the body to be lifted, and on a signal, the volunteer space cadet is gently lifted a couple of feet up, moved laterally back and forth and eventually levitated up to a maximum height (about 6'–7') and then, sooo slowly, down to a safe nonfriction landing. From lift-off to landing takes about 30 seconds.

Toward Accessibility

It is always important to ask both children and adults with disabilities if they mind being lifted from their wheelchairs. It may be easier to encourage them to transfer from their chair to the ground before beginning (a pad is helpful). Also, some people may have a bag (for urination) strapped to their leg. It's helpful to know this before-hand. Most adults will tell you where to grab.

Some participants with intellectual challenges may not have the trust to allow a high levitation — it's o.k. to stop at 2–3 feet. Challenge by Choice is a good model to follow (also see Appendix C: Safety Considerations).

For individuals who are difficult to pick up because of one condition or another (e.g., muscular dystrophy, rheumatoid arthritis), a strong blanket is an excellent prop for Levitation.

Trust Falls

p. 53, *Cowstails and Cobras II*

An effective trust exercise can be accomplished by asking a student to stand upon a stump, platform, ladder rung, etc. approximately 5 feet off the ground, and fall backward into the arms of the group. There should be at least ten to twelve individuals standing on the level ground to act as catchers.

Toward Accessibility

The photos on the following pages provide ideas for making the Trust Fall accessible to all.

Persons who use wheelchairs for mobility can participate in trust falls. The person in the left photo is staying in his chair. Spotters can position themselves in a way as to protect themselves from the chair. Also, make sure if you spot the chair, the parts you spot don't come off. The little boy on the right has cerebral palsy and uses a wheelchair for mobility. However, with some assistance, he can use the stump.

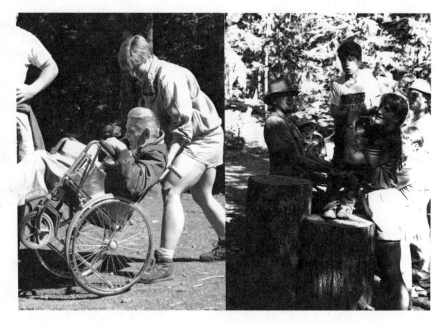

Children and adults with developmental disabilities may need more support and encouragement during the trust fall activities. It is wise to go a little slower during the sequencing of trust fall activities. However, don't assume that persons with intellectual challenges cannot learn to develop trust in themselves and others. (See photos below.)

It may be more reassuring to have a facilitator give assistance and make eye contact prior to the fall.

If persons who use crutches for support feel more comfortable using them, allow it — be sure to adjust the spotting technique.

A Word About Mutual Trust

Persons with disabilities are often asked to trust professionals in the many settings they experience. It is important for Adventure leaders to trust individuals who are disabled as they may any other participants.

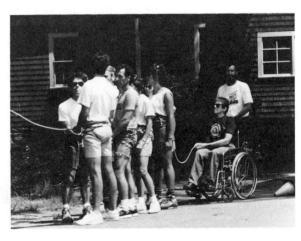

It is important to encourage all people to take responsible positions during Adventure experiences.

Initiative Problems

"Initiative exercises offer a series of clearly and often fancifully defined problems. Each task is designed so that a group must employ cooperation and some physical effort to gain a solution. Some problems are more cognitive than physical and vice-versa. This problem-oriented approach to learning can be useful in developing each individual's awareness of decision-making, leadership, and the obligations and strengths of each member within a group." (Rohnke, 1989, p. 79)

It is a general rule of thumb that if you have persons with cognitive problems, it would be helpful to choose initiative problems that are more physical; and if you have individuals with physical disabilities, the choice would be initiatives that are more mental. However, who believes in rules of thumb?

Acid River

Assemble five cinder blocks and arrange in a 1-3-1 formation. Establish boundaries on each side. The group is given two 8' lengths of 2"x6" and assigned the task of crossing the river. The blocks should be far enough apart that a lever has to be developed with the boards. Of course, there are many ways of setting up the acid river — depending on the skill level of the team. If the group has a member who touches the river or a board goes in, the team has to start over. Good luck!

Toward Accessibility

If a person has an intellectual challenge you may want to have her collaborate with another team member to assure that she provides input during the problem solving. If you have a participant who uses a wheelchair, the guidelines (rules) can be adjusted to accommodate him; e.g., one wheel can be in the acid during the crossing. If the group decides to carry the person over, it may provide for some interesting debriefing on the other side.

Sometimes the wheelchair itself becomes part of the solution.

Knots

p. 117, *Silver Bullets*

Ask a group of 10–16 individuals to face one another in a tight circle. Each person holds out his or her right hand and grasps the right hand of someone else, as if they were shaking hands. Then each person extends his or her left hand and grasps the hand of someone else, so that each person is holding two different hands. This hand-in-hand configuration should come out equal. With hands tightly held, arms intertwined and bodies juxtaposed, it's time to explain the problem. The Gordian group is to try and unwind themselves from their tangled situation so that after much try-this, try-that squirming and contorting, a hand-in-hand circle is formed. The physical hand-to-hand contact that you have with your partner cannot be broken in order to facilitate an unwinding movement.

Toward Accessibility

Be careful participants do not stumble over wheelchairs!

If persons with intellectual challenges are included, it is wise to start with a smaller group (4) until the idea is clear.

If the group has individuals with physical disabilities, you can allow people to make contact using a bandana to allow for more flexibility when untangling.

Trolley

p. 118, *Silver Bullets*

The object of this initiative problem is to move your entire group (usually 10–12) from a safe area over a designated poisoned peanut butter plot to the far side using only the provided props. A grassy area works best for safety and esthetics, but a gym floor or parking lot are also usable. If anyone touches the taboo area while trying to cross over, assign a time penalty of 15 seconds per touch. Trolley 4x4's can be as short or long as your group needs dictate.

Toward Accessibility

Participants with developmental disabilities can use a two-person trolley for practice, prior to trolleys that accommodate 8, 10, 16, etc.

People with developmental disabilities may need a more carefully sequenced approach to the trolleys. This can be accomplished by more carefully reviewing the instructions or assigning them a partner; e.g., use short two-person trolleys first with a participant and a leader on each. You can also practice the technique a few times

before getting on the trolleys or have the participants watch first.

Carabiner Walk

p. 78, Cowstails and Cobras

Have the individuals in the group tie a waistband around themselves with a sling rope. Make sure the waistband is tightly tied. Have the participants line up standing front to back and using their carabiners, clip into the waistband of the person directly in front of them. Then, instruct the group to make their way from point A to point B as quickly as possible.

Toward Accessibility

Make sure that the numbers are smaller for this activity if you include persons who use wheelchairs. Also, you may want to make sure the route you choose is free of any obstacles (you can also have webbing attached to the carabiner, so there is some distance between participants).

If people who use wheelchairs are included, it may make sense to tie one large rope around the group without having them attached to each other.

Ropes Course Elements

The key to ropes course elements is making them accessible versus adapted. The term "adapted" implies a segregated event or a situation where people do challenges that are somehow different than "normal." The term accessible implies that all participants attempt the ropes course element — "their own way." The obvious challenge is the design and construction of elements that can be challenging to a wide variety of ability levels. It is not possible, at this time, to make all elements accessible, but who knows what the future will hold. Consider the following elements.

Inclined Log

p. 50, *Cowstails and Cobras*

The inclined log is a hardwood log that is leaned on or lashed to a firm support. The student is to walk up the log in an erect posture; i.e., weight over the feet.

Toward Accessibility

This excellent beginning point on a ropes course can be made accessible by providing choices in the height and the incline of the log (beam) and the width or number of logs (beams) used. The following photos demonstrate a sample method of this accessibility.

The accessible inclined beams can be constructed to allow for a height adjustment (1'–5') and choice of one or two beams.

This participant set a goal of going up one beam backwards — this individual is visually impaired.

The participant is using one beam, walking forwards.

This participant has a developmental disability. After a goal-setting session, he decided to make the attempt using two beams.

Persons who use wheelchairs can make it up the beams as well. A pulley system can be used if the participant does not have the arm strength or balance to roll/push up the beams.

This individual has cerebral palsy. He has some difficulty walking on level ground, so he decided to make the attempt crawling up the two beams.

The preceding sequence of photos demonstrates that elements can be made accessible in a truly integrated environment. When people share the same element and develop their own style of achieving individual goals, they may begin to appreciate each other — integration does enhance acceptance.

Let's look at another element.

Swinging Log

p.108, *Cowstails an Cobras II*

The name describes this event. The 25'–30' log is suspended 8"–10" above the ground by support cables connected to the ends of the log.

Toward Accessibility

The swinging log can be made accessible through special design and construction. This kind of extra care in constructing ropes/challenge courses provide the facilitator additional "tools" for inclusive programming.

The object of the traditional swinging log is to go as far as possible from one end of the log to the other.

The accessible swinging beams allow for choices — one beam or two.

The participant on the left has chosen one beam (with eyes closed) while the child with a developmental disability set a goal of using two beams. They both, however, are challenged by the same element.

Participants who use wheelchairs can also make the attempt on the swinging beams!

High Elements

High elements can be made accessible as well. Through the use of specially designed elements and methods of assisting the person with a disability, the high ropes/challenge elements become usable. Sometimes specific elements have to be constructed. However, many high elements can be used by the participant with a disability via creativity and training.

The high accessible bridge can be a challenge for all participants. Sometimes it is good for all participants to get in the wheelchair and make the crossing.

Some Final Thoughts on Accessible Ropes Courses

As more professionals get involved in providing accessible Adventure experiences, the design and construction of elements will get more effective and efficient. Consider these innovative ideas by Schoel, Katz, and Lyle (1990):

Support mats can be used with persons who may be susceptible to pressure sores, or who need additional support.

Howie's Crossing*:* a traversing platform, suspended from cable by a ROSA Gold Pulley. Serves the function of an accessible *Nitro Crossing.*

Danny's Sling*:* a non-compressing haul system for participants who have limited use of limbs.

Zip Line Haul*:* A rope running parallel to a *Zip Wire* which enables the individual to haul him/herself with tackle to a platform.

Counterweight Climbing*:* Assists climbers in trees, walls or rope ladders who have little or no leg support.

Harnesses can be used with individuals who require additional support. This participant has spina bifida.

Do not assume that persons with physical and mental challenges cannot participate on traditional elements. All elements do not have to be accessible — just available.

Adventure Trips

There are many integrated wilderness programs available for individuals with disabilities, as mentioned earlier. Some of the most notable companies which offer accessible outdoor experiences include: Wilderness Inquiry II (Minnesota), S'PLORE (Utah), and C.W. Hog (Idaho).

These programs, in particular, offer individuals an opportunity to experience rafting, canoeing, kayaking, climbing and backpacking trips with persons of all abilities. Adventure leaders are encouraged to participate in one of these programs to learn from people with diverse physical, emotional and intellectual abilities. See Appendix A: Resource Section for details.

Technology; e.g., back supports for canoes, allows for more independent involvement with people who are disabled.

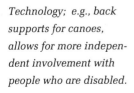

Resource Section

This appendix is divided into movies/videos, books, articles, magazines and organizations which supply the reader with resources for networking in order to more effectively serve persons who are disabled. Attention has been given to resources which provide: a) a diverse cross-section of abilities; b) insight for providing Adventure programs with persons who are disabled; and c) a focus on integration. All resources are briefly annotated.

Movies/Videos

The Able Disabled
Presents youth and young adults with disabilities participating in sports and wilderness activities. (Mendocino, CA: Lawren Productions,1980)

With A Little Help From My Friends
Conversation with nondisabled students about integration in their school. (Toronto, Can.: Vision Video Magic Concepts and Production, Ltd., 1988)

Dignity of Risk
Explores the progress of children as they participate in integrated programs. (Portland, OR: Horizon Video, 1983)

So Many Children

Documents efforts of parents and teachers in working with persons who are mentally disabled over a 20-year period. (Princeton, NJ: Films for Humanities and Sciences,1988)

Practical Suggestions For Managing Behavior

Includes strategies for managing behavior. (Oak Forest, Il: Southwest Cooperative Foundation, 1989)

Learning Disabilities

Describes cues for identifying learning disabilities. (Princeton, NJ: Films for Humanities & Sciences, 1987)

Almost Like You and Me

Normalized programming with adults who are autistic. (Rockville, MD: CC-M, 1987)

Communicating with Deaf/Blind People

Demonstrates methods of communication with deaf/blind individuals. (New York, NY: Phoenix/BFA Films, 1982)

Answering the Needs of Children with Communication Deficits

Focuses on the total communication approach to treatment. (London, Ont: Children's Psychiatric Research Institute, 1987)

Preparation for Mainstreaming

Depicts child with severe hearing loss participating in classroom activities. (Washington, DC: Alexander Graham Bell Assoc., 1981)

BOLD-Blind Outdoor Leisure Development

Presents persons who are blind participating in outdoor pursuits. (Aspen, CO: Crystal Productions, 1980)

The Mountain Does It For Me

Demonstrates how children with cerebral palsy ski. (Aspen, CO: Crystal Productions, 1981)

Seasons of Caring

Explores needs of families of young children with chronic illness. (Washington, DC: Assoc. for the Care of Children's Health, 1986)

Protect, Defend and Love-Forever

Families discuss experiences of living with person who is developmentally disabled. (Syracuse, NY: Newchannels, 1986)

As I Am: Portraits of Persons with a Developmental Handicap
Aimed at building positive attitudes towards people with developmental disabilities. (Toronto, Ont: James Brodie Productions)

Changes, Outside, & Survivors
A trilogy of films which focus on persons with spinal cord injuries. (Golden, CO: Access, Inc.)

Freedom In Depth
Film on underwater diving with persons who are disabled. (San Clemente, CA: Handicapped Scuba Association, 1990)

Education for All Children
Examines traditional attitudes towards individuals with developmental disabilities. (Champaign, Il: Research Press, 1990)

Different Approach
A humorous and effective film which advocates for the employment of persons with disabilities. (Atlanta, GA: Modern Talking Pictures)

Like Other People
Deals with the sexual, emotional and social needs of severely disabled individuals. (Northfield, IL: Perennial Education, Inc.)

Access to Parks and Recreation: Disabled People Speak
Discusses the importance of accessibility, common access problems and offers solutions. (Technical Training Videotapes, National Park Foundation, P.O. Box 57473, Washington, D.C. 20037)

Access to Parks and Recreation Facilities
Focuses on architectural/physical access to buildings, facilities, and outdoor recreation activities. (Technical Training Videotapes, National Park Foundation, P.O. Box 57473, Washington, D.C. 20037)

Books

The Child Who Never Grew
A story, written by Pearl S. Buck, about her daughter who is mentally challenged. (Buck. New York: John Day, 1950)

Down All the Days
Novel by a person who has cerebral palsy — autobiography. (Brown. Greenwich: Fawcett, 1970)

A Place for Noah
A story about a child who is autistic, written by his father, details the decisions made by the family. (Greenfield. New York:Holt, 1978)

The Story of My Life
The story of Helen Keller, who was blind — autobiography. (Keller. New York: Dell, 1954)

Deaf Like Me
Book details the struggle of a child who is deaf and his parents as they try to communicate. (Spradley. New York: Random House, 1978).

Easy Walking
Accounts young man's experience during the rehabilitation process after a spinal cord injury. (Nasaw. Philadelphia: Lippencott, 1975)

Spinal Network
Detailed book including resources, "news" and personal stories concerning persons with spinal cord injuries and related nervous system problems. (Maddox. Boulder: Spinal Network, 1990)

Human Exceptionality
Introductory textbook which includes an excellent overview of exceptionality. (Hardman, 3rd Ed. Boston: Allyn and Bacon, 1990)

Americans With Disabilities Act of 1990: Law and Explanation
A comprehensive explanation of the law using simple language. (Commerce Clearing House, Inc. Call 800–248–3248 to order and ask for catalogue #4998)

The Nonrestrictive Environment: On Community Integration for People with Disabilities
Outlines basic principles of community integration and looks at what makes it work. (Human Policy Press, P.O. Box 127, University Station, Syracuse, N.Y. 13210)

P.L. 94–142, Section 504 and P.L.99–457 — Understanding What They Are and Are Not
Answers questions about Education of the Handicapped Act and civil rights provisions of the Vocational Rehabilitation Act Amendments of

1973. (Ballard, et. al. The Council Of Exceptional Children, Dept. K 102, Reston, VA 22091–1589)

Dictionary of Special Education and Rehabilitation, 3rd Edition

Provides clear, understandable definitions of more than 2,000 terms unique to special education and rehabilitation. (Vergason, Ed. Denver: Love Publishing, Co., 1990)

Adapted Physical Education in the Mainstream, 2nd Edition

Emphasizes the special needs student in the mainstream environment. (Cratty, B. Denver: Love Publishing Co., 1990)

Specifications for Making Buildings and Facilities Accessible and Usable by Physically Handicapped People

Explains the standards for accessible buildings, homes, sidewalks, and curbs. (Free from the American National Standards Institute, 1430 Broadway, New York, N.Y. 10018)

A Guide to Designing Accessible Recreation Outdoor Recreation Facilities

Helpful information for Adventure education facilities. (Special Programs and Populations, National Park Service, Washington, D.C. 20240)

Recreation... Access in the 90's

Answers questions concerning the Americans with Disabilities Act. Offers suggestions for accessibility. (NRPA, 3101 Park Center Drive, Alexandria, VA 22302)

Articles

Dattilo, J. & Murphy, W. (1987). "Facilitating the Challenge in Adventure Recreation," Therapeutic Recreation Journal, 3rd Quarter.

Focuses on facilitating participation in Adventure recreation by providing leisure education programs that focus on knowledge of safety, awareness of resources, acquisition of activity skills, and providing knowledge related to participant opportunities.

Farbman, A. & Ellis, K. (1987). "Accessibility and Outdoor Recreation for Persons with Disabilities," Therapeutic Recreation Journal, 1st Quarter.
> Summarizes issues and recommendations in the areas of architectural accessibility, program accreditation, transportation, and involvement of disabled consumers.

Havens, M. (1990). "Make the Experience Accessible For Everyone," The Outdoor Network, Vol 1, No. 5.
> Provides a review of accessible challenge programming and makes suggestions for collaboration among companies who provide Adventure services and those that focus on accessibility.

Havens, M. (1985). "Ethical Challenges in the Outdoor Setting," Therapeutic Recreation Journal, 4th Quarter.
> Explores the ethical challenges that therapists face in the implementation of programs in the outdoor setting. The unique characteristics of this setting are contrasted with more controlled clinical environments.

Robb, G. & Ewert, A. (1987). "Risk Recreation and Persons with Disabilities," Therapeutic Recreation Journal, 1st Quarter.
> Explores the many potential benefits of risk recreation for persons who are disabled. Makes reference to the quality of current research in supporting the value of Adventure programming and provides suggestions and recommendations for including people with all abilities.

Roland, C. et. al. (1987). "Creation of an Experiential Challenge Program," Therapeutic Recreation Journal, 2nd Quarter.
> Explains how an Adventure program was designed, implemented and evaluated at a Veteran's Hospital. Reflects an interdisciplinary approach to program development focusing on social, cognitive and emotional risk-taking.

Roland, C. et. al. (1986). "Families as Partners with Disabled Youth," The Journal of Experiential Education, Summer.
> Describes the use of Adventure programming within the context of a family growth program. Explores the benefits derived from such a program through the eyes of the participants. Presents information on the effects of disability on the family system.

Smith, T. (1982). "Self-Concept, Special Populations, and Outdoor Therapy," (in G. M. Robb, Ed.), Bradford Papers Annual, Vol. II.
> Explores the theory that especially designed Adventure programs can be effective and meaningful for any comprehensive rehabilitation, counseling, recreation, or education program for persons with dis-

abilities. Provides an overall review of exceptionality and implications for the development of self-esteem.

Magazines

Mainstream
Covers a full range of topics for people with disabilities — from civil rights to aerobics. (P.O. Box 370598, San Diego, CA, 92137)

Disability Studies Quarterly
Covers a broad range of topics: women's issues, medical ethics, disability politics, etc. DSQ, Brandeis, Dept. of Sociology, Waltham, MA, 02254)

Disability Rag
This publication is about empowerment for people with disabilities. Focus on politics and "seeing" people as the way they are. (P.O. Box 145, Louisville, KY, 40201)

Accent on Living
Filled with articles about products, vocational options, leisure activities and medical news. (AOL, P.O. Box 700, Bloomington, IL, 61702)

Sports 'N Spokes
Contains news and information on competitive sports, wheelchair sports-basketball, road racing, etc. Also, includes articles on fitness, training and equipment. (5201 N. 19th Ave., Suite 111, Phoenix, AZ, 85015– 9986)

Palaestra
Includes general interest reports on topics — e.g., tennis, Outward Bound Expeditions, and climbing for people with disabilities. (Challenge publications, Ltd., P.O. Box 508, Macomb, IL, 61455)

Report on Disability Programs
Hard to find information on disability rights issues — in legislatures, courts, and government agencies. (951 Pershing Drive, Silver Springs, MD 20910– 4464)

Disabled Outdoors
Provides information on individuals with disabilities in the out-of-doors. (5223 South Lorel Ave., Chicago, IL 60638)

Organizations

Office On Americans With Disabilities Act
Provides information on Titles II, III which deal with public accommodation and commercial facilities. (Civil rights Division, US Department of Justice, P.O. Box 66118, Washington, D.C., 20035-6118).

S'PLORE
Special Populations Learning Outdoor Recreation & Education provides white water rafting trips, cross-country skiing, rock climbing, and other activities with persons who are disabled. (27 West 3300 South, SLC, UT, 84115)

C.W. HOG
Cooperative Wilderness Handicapped Outdoor Group is an Adventure based program that serves persons with all abilities. Innovations in their use of equipment has made the outdoors accessible to persons with all abilities. (ISU, Student Union, Box 8118, Pocatello, ID 83209)

Wilderness Inquiry II
Provides canoe trips, dog sledding and other wilderness experiences on an international basis. Special emphasis is on the promotion of integrated activities. (202 2nd St. N.W., #101, East Grand Forks, MN, 56271)

P.O.I.N.T.
Paraplegics On Independent Nature Trips provides nature to promote leisure and independence in such activities as backpacking, kayaking, scuba diving, boating, etc. (4101 Cummings, Bedford, TX, 76021)

B.O.E.C.
The Breckenridge Outdoor Education Center sponsors skiing, rock climbing, and other outdoor activities for persons with all abilities. (P.O. Box 697, Breckenridge, CO, 80424)

Accessible Adventures

Provides challenge education consulting, including: training, design and construction of ropes courses/playgrounds and related services concerning accessible Adventure curricula. (250 NE Tomahawk Island Drive, #309, Portland, OR, 97217)

Bradford Woods

Indiana University's Outdoor Education Center provides both outdoor programming and consultation in Adventure education with persons who are disabled. (5040 State Road 67 North, Martinsville, IN, 46151)

The Raccoon Institute

Provides consultation services in staff development and ethics training for professionals involved in Adventure education. (P.O. Box 695, Cazenovia, WI, 53924)

The American Spinal Injury Association

Provides a forum for professionals in rehabilitation to exchange information, conduct research and convene seminars and workshops. Publications can be obtained on physical medicine and rehabilitation. (250 E. Superior Street, Room 619, Chicago, IL, 60611)

Easter Seals

Has chapters throughout the United States. Through the National Office publications can be accessed on myths about disability, independent living, etc. (70 East Lake St., Chicago, IL, 60601)

The Information Center For Individuals With Disabilities, Inc.

Provides information about assistive organizations, state and federal entitlements, educational and employment resources, so disabled persons can lead more independent lives. (27– 43 Wormwood St., Boston, MA 02210)

Mainstream, Inc.

Works with both employers and disabled persons on the legal and practical aspects of job accommodation, accessibility, interviewing and recruiting. (1200 15th St. NW, Washington, DC, 20005)

The Center on Human Policy

Committed to the full inclusion of people with developmental disabilities in community life. Provides excellent information on research and training. (Syracuse University, 724 Comstock Ave., Syracuse, N.Y. 13244– 4230)

Human Policy Press

Provides resources for supporting awareness of persons with disabilities and full integration. (P.O. Box 127, University Station, Syracuse, N.Y. 13210)

National Ocean Access Project

Mission is to develop and promote sailing and marine-oriented recreational activities for individuals with disabilities. (410 Severn Ave., Suite 306, Annapolis, MD 21403)

National Park Service — Office of Special Programs and Populations

Provides information on camping and outdoor recreation with persons who are disabled. (U.S. Department of the Interior, P.O. Box 371127, Washington, D.C. 20013– 7127)

Nantahala Outdoor Center

Sponsors clinics and programs on kayaking with persons who are disabled. (Star Route, Box 68, Bryson City, NC 28713)

National Handicapped Sports and Recreation Association

Sponsor clinics and programs on outdoor sports and recreation. (1145 19th St. NW, Suite 717, Washington, D.C. 20036)

Appendix B

Self/Program/Facility Accessibility Surveys

Self-Awareness Survey

As Adventure leaders, it is imperative to begin to reflect upon personal attitudes/philosophies concerning integration. The following self-test will provide a beginning point for the reader of this primer. It may be more helpful to complete this test and discuss your responses with other colleagues, staff, friends, etc. There are no clear "right" or "wrong" answers. Appendix A: Resource Section, provides sources for additional information highlighting many of the questions in the survey.

Attitudes

1. When I've seen/read a media presentation portraying people with disabilities in negative, unproductive ways I've written a note of protest to the producer/editor/network, etc.

   ❏ Yes   ❏ No

2. When I've heard people using terms like "retard" or "cripple" I've indicated that these words are not to be included in conversations at our programs/facilities.

   ❏ Yes   ❏ No

3. Effective tool(s) in changing attitudes towards individuals with disabilities is/are:

❑ integrated Adventure activities

❑ simulations of disabilities

❑ movies

❑ information campaigns

4. Attitudes are not a concern and attitude change should not be a goal of Adventure programs.

❑ Yes   ❑ No

Legislation

1. P.L. 94– 142, which has been termed a Bill of Rights for Persons with Disabilities, mandates that individuals with disabilities be mainstreamed and deinstitutionalized.

❑ Yes   ❑ No

2. The block grant philosophy of federal support, embraced by the recent federal administration for educational aid to the states, has significantly increased monies for recreation, physical and Adventure education.

❑ Yes   ❑ No

3. Section 504 of the Rehabilitation Act of 1973, with its requirement for program accessibility, has been rigidly enforced.

❑ Yes   ❑ No

4. A.N.S.I. accessibility standards require that:

❑ ramps have a maximum gradient of 8.3% (1:12)

❑ doors be a minimum of 48" wide

❑ trails in parks/campgrounds be hard surfaced

❑ pools be equipped with ramps or lifts

Programming

1. Nearly every Adventure activity imaginable has been successfully adapted/modified for participation by individuals with disabilities.

   ❑ Yes   ❑ No

2. Neither the time nor the financial resources exist for individualized assessment and programming in community Adventure programs.

   ❑ Yes   ❑ No

3. Of the following goal structures for Adventure activities, which one works best toward acceptance of persons with disabilities?

   ❑ competitive

   ❑ cooperative

   ❑ individualistic

4. Few programming resources (activity guides, training materials, etc.) exist in the area of Adventure for persons with disabilities?

   ❑ Yes   ❑ No

5. Program standards specific to persons with disabilities have been identified in which of the following areas:

   ❑ Adventure education

   ❑ aquatics

   ❑ interscholastic athletics

   ❑ all of the above

Barriers

1. Nondisabled individuals and their parents will be turned off by the inclusion of persons with disabilities in Adventure programs.

   ❑ Yes   ❑ No

2. The costs of providing Adventure services to individuals with disabilities is prohibitive given the need for special staff ratios, equipment, transportation, insurance, etc.

   ❏ Yes   ❏ No

3. Funding for community based Adventure programming for individuals with disabilities could be generated through:

   ❏ state enabling legislation

   ❏ foundation grants/corporate gifts

   ❏ participant fees/charges

   ❏ school/rehabilitation agency monies

   ❏ inclusion in recreation department budgets

   ❏ all of the above and more

4. Training in special education or an allied health field is essential for working effectively with individuals who are disabled in Adventure programs.

   ❏ Yes   ❏ No

5. The most frequently cited barrier to effective programming for individuals identified in a national study of recreation departments was:

   ❏ special insurance/liability

   ❏ funding

   ❏ lack of personnel

   ❏ transportation

   ❏ architectural barriers

   ❏ recruitment of participants with disabilities

1. Vocational Rehabilitation Programs can provide funds and expertise for employment and training of individuals with disabilities in Adventure programs.

   ❏ Yes   ❏ No

2. The International Year Of Disabled Persons (I.Y.D.P.) had only limited national impact.

   ❏ Yes   ❏ No

3. College/university programs/students can be a major resource toward expanded community Adventure opportunities for persons with disabilities.

   ❏ Yes   ❏ No

(Adapted from Witman, J. & Powell, L. (1983). *Attitudes: Barriers or Enabler of Full Recreational Participation for Individuals with Disabilities.* University of New Hampshire, Durham, NH, Project PAR)

*Note: If after reading this primer and consulting the other appendices, you still have questions regarding this self-test, discuss the content with persons who are disabled and professionals in the fields of special education and rehabilitation to further your awareness/knowledge level.

Program Survey

Surveys are available for program and facility accessibility (see Appendix A: Resource Section). Consider using a survey as a self-evaluation of your Adventure programs' services and facilities. The surveys, included in this appendix, are not intended to replace obligations you may have with reference to the Americans With Disabilities Act (1990) or Section 502 and Section 504 of the Rehabilitation Act (1973). In order to make this process more effective, consider:

• Inviting a person who has a disability to review program and facility accessibility with you;

- Asking a professional, who represents persons with disabilities and is knowledgeable about the Uniform Accessibility Standards (UFAS), to assist you;

- Obtaining a copy of the Section 502– 504 requirements and the UFAS Standards along with the new ADA Standards and using them to determine program/facility accessibility; and

- Checking your state requirements for accessibility (these standards are often more strict than federal).

Answers to the following questions will help evaluate your program

- Do you actively advertise and recruit persons with disabilities to your programs?

- Do you ensure effective communication with persons who are disabled (e.g. interpreters, large print, raised print)?

- Do you have adequately trained staff to include persons with disabilities in your programs, safely and effectively?

- Is there a process in place for insuring confidentiality of information on participants?

- Do you have consultants to assist with modifying activities and services for persons with different abilities (e.g. physical therapist, occupational therapist, therapeutic recreation specialist)?

- Do you have an orientation and follow-up program in place for participants?

- Do you have a training program for staff which focuses on successfully including persons with disabilities in program activities and services?

- Do your program manuals address activity modification procedures, facilitation strategies, safety requirements, etc. to ensure effective participation by persons who are disabled?

- Do you have adequate communication with persons who are disabled, e.g., hearing impaired, to inform them of policy and schedule changes?

- Do you have a policy in place which informs all parties (Board of Directors, Staff, Consumers, etc.) that your agency does not discriminate against persons who are disabled?

Facility Survey

- Is the ground graded so that it is level with the normal entrance in and around your ropes/challenge course area (including areas for such activities as trust building, awareness, cooperative play, etc.)?

- Are entrance ways to program areas at least 48 inches wide and have a gradient not greater than five percent?

- Are there parking spaces that are accessible and approximate to the facilities and program areas which have been set aside and identified for individuals with mobility problems?

- If you have ramps leading to and from program areas or in and out of buildings, is the slope not greater than a one foot rise in 12 feet, or 8.33 percent, or four degrees 40 minutes?

- Is at least one entrance to each building used accessible to individuals who use wheelchairs for mobility?

- Do the doors on the facilities used open to a minimum of 32 inches and are they operable by a single effort?

- Do the stairs in and around buildings have risers that do not exceed seven inches?

- Do floors and ropes/challenge course elements have some surfaces that are "nonslip?"

- Are there mirrors in some of the laboratories that are no higher than 40 inches above the floor (measured from the top of the shelf and the bottom of the mirror)?

- Do the water fountains or coolers have up front spouts and controls?

- Is there a phone which is equipped for persons who are hearing impaired with instructions?

- Are controls for light, heat, ventilation, windows, draperies, fire alarms, etc. within the reach of persons who use wheelchairs?

- Do you have raised letters and numbers to identify rooms, offices, and ropes/challenge course elements?

- Are handrails available on some walkways (particularly if ramps or walkways are steeper than a five percent gradient rise)?

- Are the ramps at least 36 inches wide?

- Are there edges to ramps or bridges which will help individuals from slipping off?

- Is carpet in and around buildings securely attached?

- Do restrooms have a turning space 60x60 inches; a stall that is three feet wide, four feet eight inches deep; a door that swings 32 inches wide; a handrail on each side (33 inches high, parallel to the floor, 1 1/2 inches in diameter, 1 1/2 inches between rail and wall and fastened securely to the wall); has a toilet seat of 17–19 inches from the stand?

- Are there tables available 27 inches high, 30 inches wide and 19 inches deep for knee clearance and is the table top 28–34 inches from the floor?

Sources for Additional Surveys

Access Oregon
2600 S.E. Belmont Street, Suite A
Portland, OR 97214

Community Recreation and Persons with Disabilities
Schleien & Ray (1988) Baltimore: Brooks Publishing Co. (Appendix F)

Appendix C

Safety Considerations

Assisting a Person Who Has a Seizure

1. Ease the person to the floor and loosen the collar. You will not be able to stop the seizure. Let it happen and do not try and revive the individual.

2. Remove hard, sharp, or hot objects that may injure the person. However, do not interfere with movements of the individual.

3. Don't force anything between the teeth. If the mouth is open, place a soft object — a handkerchief — between the back teeth. Be careful not to get your fingers between the person's teeth.

4. Turn the person's head to one side for the release of saliva. Place something soft underneath the head.

5. When the individual regains consciousness, let him rest — if he wishes.

6. If the seizure lasts beyond a few minutes, or if the person seems to pass from one seizure to another without gaining consciousness, call for medical assistance. Also, make sure onlookers are told to vacate the area. One or two leaders can deal with the situation.

Identifying Decubitus Ulcers (Pressure Sores)

People with spinal cord injuries can be susceptible to pressure sores or decubitus ulcers. Adults, who have been injured for awhile, are experts in avoiding such problems. You will notice people who use wheelchairs shifting about and moving often to avoid pressure to a specific area. Children, however, may need to be reminded to take caution in the prevention of pressure sores.

1. A pressure sore can result from any one or a combination of pressure, heat, moisture and friction.

2. Insulite pads should be available at all times during Adventure programs; also, take care to alleviate friction at all times on ropes/challenge course. Opportunities to "dry out" should be scheduled into the day if wet conditions exist.

3. A red area or other indication of tissue deterioration such as swelling and heat are indicators of a sign of any decubitus.

4. If the discoloration does not fade within a reasonable time (15 to 30 minutes), take precautions to avoid further pressure to the area.

5. An adult with a disability will be the best source of information related to pressure sores. If you feel comfortable, ask her to make recommendations regarding your Adventure equipment and programs to prevent such problems.

6. With children, it is important to remind them about pressure sores and have medical personnel who are familiar with proper treatment.

Good Lifting, Carrying and Lowering Mechanics

To Lift

- Plan the job.

- Make sure there is room for good footing and the path is cleaned for the carry.

- Stand so you will not have to twist as you lift.

- Face the person squarely, with your feet close to him, and spaced apart about the width of your hips.

- Do not try to lift from a kneeling position — with the knee touching the floor. This takes away from the power source.

- Get a good handhold before starting the lift.

- Make a preliminary lift to see if the person is within your capacity.

- If the weight of the person is more than one-fourth of your body weight, get someone else to assist you.

- Get your legs ready for the lift by bending them. Do not attempt with the legs bent beyond the right angle position.

- The back should be straight, and maybe far from a vertical position as long as the back is not arched. Keep your back steady.

- The shoulders should be directly over the knees and the hands should reach straight downward to the person.

- When you are in proper position, your leg muscles are ready to go to work while your back muscles are holding your back steady.

- Lift by straightening the legs in a steady upward thrust and, at the same time, move the back to a vertical position.

- The weight of the person should be kept close to your body and over your feet.

- As your legs are straightened, keep your back straight.

- To change direction during the lift, step around and turn your whole body without twisting.

- Lower your body to the near level of the person to be lifted to carry.

To Carry

- Carry the person as close to you as possible.

- Keep a firm grasp.

- If the grasp becomes loose, rest the person firmly against something while you secure a firmer grip or put him down.

- Keep your back straight, not arched.

- Do not twist, change direction by stepping around and turning the whole body.

To Lower

- Make sure there is ample room for good footing.

- Make sure your grasp is firm before lowering the person.

- Spread your legs to hip width and lower the load to between your feet.

- Hold your back straight and steady, even when you lean forward.

- Lower in a slow and even manner by bending your legs.

- Extend your arms straight downward and keep the load close to your body.

- Do not twist your body. To turn, move your feet.

(Adapted from, **Parent Aid Series**, "Assisting the Cerebral Palsied Child Lifting and Carrying." United Cerebral Palsy Association, 66 East 34th Street, New York, NY.)

Sequencing Adventure Activities

There are many opinions and methods for sequencing Adventure activities. Resources which will provide guidance in this area include:

Robb, et. al. (1983). *Special Education...Naturally.* Bradford Woods, 5040 State Road 67 N., Martinsville, IN 46151.

Schoel, S. et. al. (1988). *Islands of Healing.* Project Adventure, Inc., Hamilton, MA 01936.

Roland, C. & et. al. (1987). Creation of an experiential challenge program. *Therapeutic Recreation Journal*, 2nd Quarter.

Logistical Considerations

To assure that integrated Adventure experiences are conducted safely and effectively in your particular setting, consider the following factors:

Time

How much time do you have to spend with each group? An important factor in selecting the challenge level for the group or individual is how well you know the participants. If you have time to offer a sequence of activities you have a chance to assess the risk taking propensity of the group or individual. The more time, the better. Be realistic about what you can offer a group depending upon the amount of time you have to spend with them. Focus on the process not the product.

Personnel

Set specific goals for the integrated group. Focus on your limitations and abilities as leaders. Offer only those experiences that you are trained to implement. Your goals for the group should be consistent with your expertise.

Resources

It helps to have an interdisciplinary group of facilitators. If your agency serves a variety of user groups, the facilitator with the most experience with a particular group should be the lead facilitator.

The following techniques are used at the Mt. Hood Kiwanis Camp (Oregon) to assess the physical and emotional abilities of campers. They are simple techniques, however, they have proven effective in assessing the readiness of individual participants who are disabled.

Camper Reactions at the Challenge Course

Name of Camper _____

Name of Supervisor _____

Dates _____

Week: 1 2 3 4 5 6 7 8 (Circle)

Name of Rater _____

Rating Codes

1 = cries
2 = frowns
3 = smiles
4 = laughs
5 = no affect

Element	Start	During	After
Inclined Balance Beam	1 2 3 4 5	1 2 3 4 5	1 2 3 4 5
2nd attempt	1 2 3 4 5	1 2 3 4 5	1 2 3 4 5
Scoot Bridge	1 2 3 4 5	1 2 3 4 5	1 2 3 4 5
2nd attempt	1 2 3 4 5	1 2 3 4 5	1 2 3 4 5
Hickory Jump	1 2 3 4 5	1 2 3 4 5	1 2 3 4 5
2nd attempt	1 2 3 4 5	1 2 3 4 5	1 2 3 4 5
Wild Woosey	1 2 3 4 5	1 2 3 4 5	1 2 3 4 5
2nd attempt	1 2 3 4 5	1 2 3 4 5	1 2 3 4 5
Wall	1 2 3 4 5	1 2 3 4 5	1 2 3 4 5
2nd attempt	1 2 3 4 5	1 2 3 4 5	1 2 3 4 5

Instructions

Each participant is coded at the start, during, and after each element (a second attempt is also provided). The number is circled based on the facial expression of the camper — many of the participants are nonverbal. 1 = cries and 2 = frowns are considered "anxiety" gestures; 3 = smiles and 4 = laughs are considered "non-anxiety" gestures. If a camper exhibits a sequence of 3's and 4's before, during, and after the element, she is considered "ready" for the next level of challenge (note: this is a very subjective evaluation, however, it does provide the leader with additional information).

Camper Performance at the Challenge Course

Name of Camper _____

Name of Supervisor _____

Dates _____

Week: 1 2 3 4 5 6 7 8 (circle)

Name of Rater _____

Rating Codes

        1 = total assistance needed

        2 = partial assistance needed

        3 = achieves independently

Elements (Sample)

Inclined Balaxnce Beam	one beam 4" side	1 2 3
	one beam 6" side	1 2 3
	two beams	1 2 3
	other	1 2 3
Burma Bridge	walks forward	1 2 3
	crawls forward using mat	1 2 3
	walks backwards	1 2 3
	other	1 2 3
Tire Traverse	swings from tire to tire	1 2 3
	walks tire to tire on board	1 2 3
	crawls on board through tires	1 2 3
	other	1 2 3

Instructions

Each camper is evaluated on his or her ability to accomplish the chosen method of solving an element. After the campers achieve their goal, which may involve partial assistance, they go to the next element (campers are encouraged to decide for themselves when it is time to move on).

Appendix D

Key Definitions and Terms

Definitions

Challenge By Choice
A concept used by Project Adventure which encourages all participants to choose their own level of involvement including physical, intellectual and emotional in Adventure experiences.

Full-Value Contract
An process used at Project Adventure which sets the tone for groups involved in Adventure experiences. This process urges the participants to establish guidelines for working as a group; e.g., the group members agree that no one will discount another.

Disability
Generally, refers to the reduced function or loss of a particular body part or organ.

Exceptional
Usually refers to any child whose physical attributes and/or learning abilities differ from the "norm." Can be above or below, enough so that an individualized program of special education is required (IEP).

Handicap
These include problems a person who is disabled has when interacting with the environment.

Impairment

Can imply disease, damage or defective tissue. This term is used synonymously with disability.

Qualified Person

Under the Americans with Disabilities Act, anyone possessing a physical or mental impairment that substantially limits one or more major life activities, anyone with a record of such impairment, or anyone regarded as having an impairment.

Terms

American National Standards Institute (ANSI)

A private organization which develops specifications in a variety of areas, including building and design construction. It publishes, *Specifications for Making Buildings and Facilities Accessible to and Usable by Physically Handicapped Persons.*

Barrier-Free Environment

An environment that contains no obstacles to accessibility and usability by persons with disabilities. Barriers may exist under section 504 so long as they do not impede program accessibility. Rules related to new construction and alterations do apply when constructed with federal funds.

Equal Opportunity

Translates into achievement of accessibility, the provision of benefits, services and aids that are effective for handicapped and non-handicapped people, and programs and activities that are otherwise free from discrimination based on handicap.

Individuals With Handicaps

A person who has a physical or mental impairment that substantially limits one or more major life activities (e.g. caring for oneself, performing manual tasks, walking, seeing, hearing, speaking, breathing, learning and working); has a record of such an impairment (has a history of, or has been misclassified as having, a mental or physical impairment that substantially limits one or more major life activities); or, is regarded as having such an impairment.

Qualified Handicapped Person

With respect to employment, is a person with a disability who, with reasonable accommodation, can perform the essential functions of the job in question and with respect to services, a person with a disability who meets the essential eligibility requirements for the receipt of such services.

Readily Achievable

Under the ADA Act, public accommodations must remove architectural and communication barriers if removal is readily achievable — without undue hardship (alternative options can be explored).

Reasonable Accommodation

The principle by which a recipient's employment practices are to be made accessible to qualified persons with disabilities. Agencies are required to make certain adjustments to the known physical and mental limitations of otherwise qualified applicants/employees who are disabled, unless it can be demonstrated that a particular adjustment or alteration would impose undue hardship on the operation of the program.

Recipient

Any state or its political subdivision, an instrumentality of a state or its political subdivision, any public or private agency, institution, organization, or other entity, or any person to which federal financial assistance is extended directly, or through another recipient, including any successor, assignee or transfer of a recipient, but excluding the ultimate beneficiary of the assistance.

Ultimate Beneficiary

As opposed to a recipient, is the employee, student, patient or other individual who receives the end result of the federally funded program.

Undue Hardship

A recipient shall make accommodation to the known physical or mental limitations of an otherwise qualified person with a disability who is an applicant or employee unless the recipient can demonstrate that such accommodation would impose undue hardship on the operation of its program. However, the regulations to date provide no precise criteria for determining undue hardship.

Appendix E

Sample Resources For Training

Learning from Individuals with Disabilities

A process for getting to know a person with a disability can be initiated through an interview. The following questions can serve as an outline for interviewing a person with a disability. Remember, use it as a guideline and be sincere in asking the questions which may be important to you. Also, it would be less intimidating to arrange for an interview through a friend, family member or one of the organizations listed in Appendix A: Resource Section.

Outline

1. What is your personal definition of adventure?

2. In what ways do you take risks or challenge yourself?

3. How can I, as a leader, use language which is not offensive to persons with disabilities?

4. What are the most significant barriers to accessibility in the work, community, recreation, and Adventure (you may have to explain your field of practice) settings?

5. What impact will the Americans With Disabilities Act (ADA) have on society (and/or Adventure programs)?

6. Are there other laws or legislative actions that I should be aware of?

7. Are there resources (books, movies, etc.) which would help me be more aware and accepting of persons who have disabilities?

8. What is your personal definition of accessibility?

9. What other questions should I be asking in order to be more able to program with people who have different abilities?

10. Other questions important to you:

_____

_____

_____

Sample Resources For In-Service Training

There are several in-service training programs available for Adventure leaders who desire to heighten their own (and their staff's) awareness, skills and knowledge for working with persons who are disabled. Specialists are often eager to assist professionals who intend to integrate their programs/facilities. A place to begin is with one of the following allied health professional organizations (these listed represent only a few of the many organizations available):

National Therapeutic Recreation Society
3101 Park Center Drive
Alexandria, VA 22302-1593

The American Physical Therapy Association
1111 North Fairfax Street
Alexandria, VA 22314

The American Occupational Therapy Association
1383 Picard Drive
Rockville, MD 20850

Council For Exceptional Children
1920 Association Drive
Reston, VA 22091-1589

The Association for the Severely Handicapped
1070 Roosevelt Way NE
Seattle, WA 98115

Check your state Independent Living Association for assistance from people with disabilities.

These state and national offices will assist you in identifying local resources for assistance. Individuals from these associations will consult with you on program development, accessibility considerations and in-service training.

The federal government has funded numerous projects over the past five years which focus on training personnel in working with persons who are disabled. Listed and annotated below are several projects which have produced curricula or are in the process of doing so:

The Leisure Integration Through Community Partnerships (LITCP) Project was instituted in 1986 with funds from the United States Department of Education. The LITCP Project was designed to minimize barriers to community integration for persons with disabilities. A guide and additional materials are available from the Ability Center, 5605 Monroe Street, Sylvannia, Ohio 43560.

Integration Through Outdoor Recreation Partnerships is a new project funded by the Department of Education. The primary purpose of the project is to develop, demonstrate and disseminate a leisure model that will enable adults with severe disabilities to participate in mainstreamed outdoor recreation programs. Products from this project will include outdoor recreation skills and awareness training curricula. The materials will be available from Portland State University, Special Education Program, PO Box 751, Portland, Oregon 97207.

Closing The Gap is a manual, funded by the federal government, that promotes community integration. It provides advice for agencies which are serious about changing policies and procedures to include all persons in their programs. Available from San Jose State University, Department of Leisure Studies, San Jose, California 95192.

LIFE: Leisure is for Everyone is a curriculum developed to accompany a two day training program for community recreation professionals. Prepares participants to return to their community parks and recreation agencies and train other personnel in techniques to integrate persons with disabilities into their programs. Available from the University of North Carolina, Curriculum in Recreation Administration, Chapel Hill, North Carolina.

Access Indiana is a project designed to provide training for park and recreation agencies in Indiana to make their programs physically and programmatically accessible to persons with disabilities; and to provide direct recreation services with persons with disabilities in community recreation agencies and in the Indiana State Park System. Information will be available from Bradford Woods Outdoor Center, 5040 State Road 67 North, Martinsville, Indiana, 46151.

Sample Exercises

Exercise I: Integrative Realities:

The following case studies represent problems or situations which may be encountered when integrating Adventure programs. These situations are "real" cases and are most effective if analyzed by your staff and/or administration and discussed in order to prepare for proaction. It may also be helpful to review these cases with individuals who are disabled and professionals in special education and other related fields.

Case 1   George A., a special educator in your community, calls to question your expertise in serving students with disabilities. He states that your community Adventure program, which involves mentally challenged individuals, does not teach the kids anything and undoes a lot of the behavior controls which have been established at the school. He concludes by saying, "after all, none of your staff is trained to the extent we teachers are." How will you respond?

Case 2   You've made a decision to integrate a number of children with disabilities into your weekend Adventure program. Several of the parents of the able-bodied children call the office and threaten to pull their child out of the program. How do you respond?

Case 3.　Georgette, a 15-year-old camper with cerebral palsy is the focus of many jokes and apparently the friend of no one on an extended Adventure trip. During the second day of the trip, you as the leader, receive a complaint from one of Georgette's tentmates that the trip is really rotten compared to last year because she spent all day waiting for the "crippled" kid. Also, you get a tearful request from Georgette, who wants to go home. What is your response to each person involved?

Case 4.　Your supervisor/board of directors have determined that it would be a good policy to hire a person with a disability as a staff member. They request your input regarding, a) the types of positions you feel he or she would be most successful at; and b) the specific disabilities (e.g. deaf, blind, mentally retarded) you would exclude from the process. What is your response?

(Adapted from notes acquired from Gary M. Robb, 1980)

Exercise II: Taking a Closer Look

- Pass out oranges or apples to the group (even river rocks have been used for this one).

- Tell the participants not to eat the "goods" yet. Have them describe their fruit with as many "one-word" adjectives as possible – "see the orange, be the orange." Give them ten minutes.

- Have them place the fruit back into a bag — all together. Watch out, they get pretty attached to their apple/orange/rock. Give the bag a shake. Now, pour out the objects and have them find their piece of fruit by careful observation.

- Once they all have found the "their" object, instruct them to write a story about their new found object using all of the "one-word" adjectives in the story. Have them read their stories to the group – Remember, challenge by choice!

- Follow-up the stories with questions regarding: What does this activity have to do with persons who are disabled? Labels? Stereotypes? – importance of looking at all people as individuals. This activity can enhance the leaders overall ability to be an effective observer.

Exercise III: Follow the Star

- Use the star provided below by xeroxing several copies (enlarging is permitted). You will need several small compact mirrors.

- Instruct the group to break into teams of four. The object is to place the mirror, in a upright position, facing the star – where indicated on diagram. The participant has one minute to trace, inside the lines, around the star looking only in the mirror for reference. The other three group members rate the participants' performance on a 1–10 scale (10 being superb) — scores are averaged and participant is given the results by the group. Each member in the group of four takes a turn.

- Following the activity, appropriate questions may include; How did you like having a time constraint? How did you like being evaluated by your peers? What did the activity bring up for you? Frustration? Anger? Stress? Challenge? Fun? Something else? Some people may suggest that this activity simulates a learning disability — dyslexia.

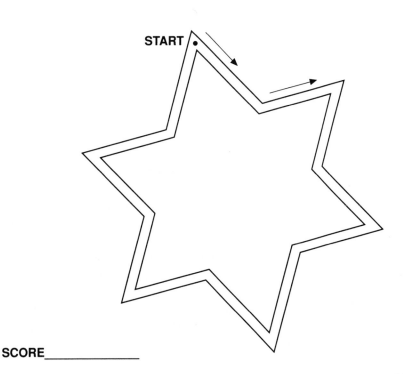

Place mirror on end along this line

START

SCORE_____

Bibliography

Bowe, F. (1978). **Handicapping America**. New York: Harper & Rowe.

Bower, E. (Ed.). (1980). **The Handicapped in Literature**. Denver: Love Publishing Company.

Brinker, R. P. (1985). Interactions between severely mentally retarded students and other students in integrated and segregated public school settings. **American Journal of Mental Deficiency**, 89, 587– 594.

Connolly, P. & Peterson, C. (1978). **Characteristics of Special Populations**. Hawkins & Associates, 804 "D" St. N.E., Washington, D.C., 20002.

Csiksentmihalyi, M. (1975). **Beyond Boredom and Anxiety**. San Francisco: Jossey-Bass.

DeLoach, C. & Greer, G. (1981). **Adjustment to Severe Physical Disability.** New York: McGraw-Hill Book Company.

Donder, D., & Nietupski, J. (1981). Nonhandicapped adolescents teaching playground skills to their mentally handicapped peers. Toward a less restrictive middle school environment. **Education and Training of the Mentally Retarded**, 16, 270– 276.

Funk, R. (1986). Lou Harris reached out and touched the Disabled Community. **Mainstream**, May.

Guralink, D. (Ed.). (1978). **Webster's New World Dictionary** (2nd Ed.). William Collins-World Publishing Co., Inc.

Grossman, H. J. (Ed.) (1983). **Manual on Terminology and Classification in Mental Retardation**. Washington, D.C.: American Association on Mental Deficiency.

Hanak, M. & Scott A. (1983). **Spinal Cord Injury**. New York: Springer Publishing Company.

Handicapped Requirements Handbook. (1990). Baltimore: Thompson Publishing Company.

Hardman, M. et. al. (1990). **Human Exceptionality** (3rd Ed.). Boston: Allyn & Bacon.

Haring, N. & McCormack, L. (Eds.). (1990). **Exceptional Children and Youth.** Columbus: Merrill Publishing Company.

Heward, W. & Orlansky, M. (1988). **Exceptional Children**. Columbus, OH: Merrill Publishing Company.

Howe-Murphy, R. & Charboneau, B. (1987). **Therapeutic Recreation Intervention: An Ecological Perspective**. Englewood Cliffs: Prentice-Hall, Inc.

Kirk, S. & Gallagher, J. (1989). **Educating Exceptional Children**. Boston: Houghton Mifflin Company.

Maddox, S. (1990). **Spinal Network**. PO Box 4162, Boulder, CO 80306.

Network News. Boston University, School of Education, Boston, MA. Summer, 1990.

Patterson, J. (1988). Chronic illness in children and the impact on families. In C. Chilman, et. al. (Eds.), **Chronic Illness and Disability: Families in Trouble** (Vol. 2), (pp. 69– 107). Newbury Park, CA.: Sage Publications.

Robb, et. al. (1983). **Special Education...Naturally**. Bradford Woods, 5040 State Road 67 N., Martinsville, IN 46151.

Rohnke, K. (1977). **Cowstails and Cobras**. Hamilton, MA: Project Adventure.

Rohnke, K. (1984). **Silver Bullets**. Hamilton, MA: Project Adventure.

Rohnke, K. (1988). **The Bottomless Bag**. Hamilton, MA: Project Adventure.

Rohnke, K. (1989). **Cowstails and Cobras II**. Hamilton, MA: Project Adventure.

Roos, P. (1982). Special trends and issues. In P.T. Cegelka & H.J. Prehm (Eds.), **Mental Retardation: From Categories to People**. Columbus, Ohio: Charles E. Merrill Publishing Co.

Schleien, S. & Ray, T. (1988). **Community Recreation and Persons with Disabilities**. Baltimore: Paul H. Brooks Publishing Co.

Schoel, S. et. al. (1988). **Islands of Healing**. Project Adventure, Inc., Hamilton, MA 01936.

Spinal Cord Society Newsletter. Seaman, J. & DePauw, K. (1989). **The New Adapted Physical Education** (2nd Ed.). Mountain View, CA: Mayfield Publishing Company.

The Ability Center (1988). **Focus on Abilities: A Guide to Including Persons with Disabilities in Community Recreation Programs.** 5605 Monroe St., Sylvania, OH, 43560.

Smith, T. (1990). **Wilderness Beyond...Wilderness Within**. Raccoon Institute, Box 695, Cazenovia, WI 53924.

U.S. Bureau of the Census (1985). **Current Population Reports**. (Series P-60, No. 149), Washington D.C.: U.S. Government Printing Office.

U.S. Department of Health, Education and Welfare. (1977). **The Federal Register**. 42, No. 163.

Wolfensberger, W. (1972). **Normalization: Principles of Normalization in Human Services**. Toronto: National Institute of Mental Retardation.

Wolfensberger, W. (1985). "An Overview of Social Role Valorization and Some Reflections on Elderly Mentally Retarded Persons," in Janicki & Wisniewski, (Eds.), **Aging and Developmental Disabilities Issues and Approaches**. Baltimore: Paul H. Brooks Publishing Company.

Photography Credits

The following photographers have contributed the photographs for this book. The page numbers where their photos appear are listed after each name.

Mark Havens
pp. 33 (bottom), 67, 86, 87 (bottom right), 89 (top right)

Cynthia Holland
pp. 26, 27, 33 (top), 40 (bottom), 68 (both), 72 (top), 88 (bottom), 89 (top left)

Carolyn Quinn
p. 4

Erik Marter
pp. 5, 21, 28, 34, 38 (bottom), 47, 70, 74 (top), 80 (all), 81 (top left), 85, 87 (top left), 88 (top)

Joanne Maynard
p. 6

photos courtesy of Pam McPhee, University of New Hampshire
pp. 11, 12

Don Rogers
p. 14

Jonie Swift
pp. 71, 82, 83 (top)

Tom Zierk
pp. 55, 56, 57, 61, 81 (bottom right)

Photographs appearing in the book but not listed above are from unknown photographers. If you can identify any of these, or if any belong to you, please contact Tom Zierk at Project Adventure, Inc.

Project Adventure Services and Publications

Services

Project Adventure, Inc. is a national, non-profit corporation dedicated to helping schools, agencies, and others implement Project Adventure programs. Toward that end, the following services are available:

Project Adventure Workshops. Through a network of national certified trainers, Project Adventure conducts workshops for teachers, counselors, youth workers and other professionals who work with people. These workshops are given in various sections of the country. Separate workshops are given in Challenge Ropes Course Skills, Counseling Skills for Adventure Based Programs, Project Adventure Games and Initiatives, and Interdisciplinary Academic Curriculum.

Challenge Course Design and Installation. Project Adventure has been designing and installing ropes courses (a series of individual and group challenge elements situated indoors in a gymnasium or outdoors in a grove of trees) for over 15 years. PA Staff can travel to your site and design/install a course appropriate for your needs and budget.

Challenge Ropes Course Source Book. A catalog service of hard-to-find materials and tools used in the installation of Challenge Ropes Courses. This catalog also contains climbing rope and a variety of items useful to adventure programs.

Executive Reach. Management workshops for business and professional persons. These workshops are designed for increasing efficiency of team members in the workplace. The trust, communication, and risk-taking ability learned in the executive programs translate into a more cohesive and productive team at work.

Program Accreditation. The Accreditation process is an outside review of a program by PA staff. Programs that undertake the accreditation process are seeking outside evaluation with regard to quality and safety. The term accreditation means "formal written confirmation." Programs seeking confirmation are looking to ensure that they are within the current standards of safety and risk management. This assurance may be useful for making changes in program equipment and/or design, and in providing information on program quality to third parties such as administrators, insurance companies and the public.

Publications

If you would like to obtain additional copies of this book, an order form is provided on the next page. Project Adventure also publishes many books and pamphlets in related areas. Described below are some of our best sellers, which can be ordered on the same form. Call or write to Project Adventure for a complete publications list.

Cowstails and Cobras II. Karl Rohnke's classic guide to games, Initiative problems and Adventure activities. Offering a thorough treatment of Project Adventure's philosophy and approach to group activities, *Cowstails II* provides both the experienced practitioner and the novice with a unique and valuable resource.

Silver Bullets. More Initiative problems, Adventure games and trust activities from Karl Rohnke: 165 great games and activities that require few, if any, props. Use this as a companion to *Cowstails and Cobras II* or a stand alone guide to invigorate your program.

Project Adventure Safety Manual. An Instructor's guide for Initiatives and High and Low Elements, this practical, hands-on and detailed manual is designed to aid those in the field running Adventure programs that utilize a challenge ropes course. The manual provides, in outline form, the standards needed for Project Adventure's program accreditation but presents the information in such a way that it can be used by anyone working with a ropes course in their program. Included are task descriptions and instructor's, participant's and spotter's roles for 14 Initiatives, 11 Low Elements and 14 High Elements. Also included are sections detailing standards for belaying, ropes course set-up, accepted equipment and more. Use of this manual ensures that all persons involved in the running of a ropes course are doing so in an accepted and consistent manner.

Silver Bullets Video. This first of its kind video presents Karl leading 20 of the best Project Adventure games and Initiatives. The video guides viewers through the events as Karl presents instructions, variations, safety tips, unique ways to choose sides, implementation help, and insights that come from doing these events for 20 years. The video goes beyond what the books can do because you actually see the games played out — from beginning to often riotous end. Also included is a field manual that outlines rules, goals, safety considerations and leadership issues that present different perspectives to each event. Running time: 2:05

Islands Of Healing: A Guide to Adventure Based Counseling, presents a comprehensive discussion of this rapidly growing counseling approach. Started in 1974, ABC is an innovative, community-based, group counseling model that uses cooperative games, Initiative problem solving, low and high Challenge Ropes Course elements, and other Adventure activities. The book contains extensive "how-to" information on group selection, training, goal setting, sequencing, and leading and debriefing activities. Also included are explorations of model ABC programs at several representative sites — junior and senior high schools, a psychiatric hospital, and court referred programs. By Jim Schoel, Dick Prouty, and Paul Radcliffe.

Order/Request Form

Please send information on the following programs:

❏ Project Adventure Training Workshops
❏ Challenge Course Design & Installation
❏ Ropes Course Equipment Catalog
❏ Executive Reach Programs
❏ Publications List
❏ Program Accreditation
❏ Please add my name to your mailing list

Please send the following books:

Qty	Title	Price	Total
	Cowstails and Cobras II	$18.50	
	Silver Bullets	$18.50	
	Bridges to Accessibility	$12.00	
	PA Safety Manual	$12.00	
	Silver Bullets Video	$44.95	
	Islands of Healing	$20.50	

Subtotal _____

5% tax (Mass. residents only) _____

Shipping (instructions below) _____

Total _____

Shipping Instructions

Orders up to $35.00 — add $3.50

Orders over $35.00 add 10% of total

(Canada & overseas, add additional $2.00 to total)

Ship to:

Name _____

Street _____

City _____ State _____ Zip _____

Phone (_____) _____

Payment:

❏ Check enclosed   ❏ Purchase Order
(For institutions only, over $25.00.)

Charge to:

❏ MasterCard   ❏ Visa

Card # _____

Exp. Date _____

Signature _____
(signature required for all credit cards)

Copy or detach this form and return to:

Project Adventure, Inc.
P.O. Box 100
Hamilton, MA 01936
508/468-7981 • FAX 508/468-7605

or

P.O. Box 2447
Covington, GA 30209
404/784-9310 • FAX 404/787-7764